Those Glorious Days

A History of Louisville
as Georgia's Capital, 1796–1807

The Old Market House or Slave Market
Louisville, Georgia, built circa 1796

Those Glorious Days

A History of Louisville
as Georgia's Capital, 1796–1807

Yulssus Lynn Holmes

Mercer University Press
Macon, Georgia

ISBN 0-86554-527-8   MUP/P149

Those Glorious Days
A History of Louisville as Georgia's Capital, 1796–1807

by Yulssus Lynn Holmes

Copyright 1996
Mercer University Press
Macon, Georgia 31210

Library of Congress Cataloging-in-Publication Data

Holmes, Yulssus Lynn, 1940–
      Those glorious days : a history of Louisville as Georgia's
capital, 1796–1807 / Yulssus Lynn Holmes.
      viii + 128 pp.   6 x 9"(15 x 23 cm.)
      Includes bibliographical references and index.
      ISBN 0-86554-527-8 (alk. paper)
      1. Louisville (Ga.)—History.   2. Georgia—Capital and
capitol—History. I. Title.
F294.L65H65   1996
975.8'663—dc20   96–30440
                                                         CIP

Contents

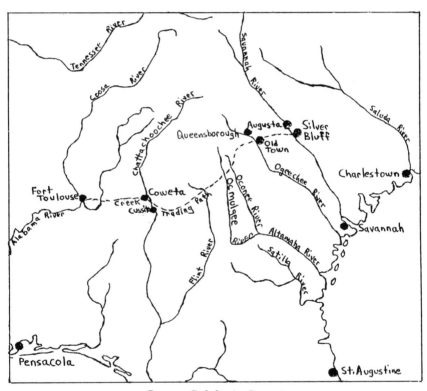

George Galphin's Georgia

Preface

After my parents, Mr. and Mrs. Y. H. Holmes, moved to Louisville, Georgia, in 1967, I began to take an interest in that town, even though I never really lived there. As a professional ancient historian, I found myself intrigued by the importance of this historic place, although I really knew nothing about its history or the history of Georgia in general. Around 1970, I decided to learn something about early Louisville and to remove some of my ignorance about Georgia history as well. My quest led me to an extensive amount of material on this fascinating town, and to my surprise I discovered that the books about this Georgia capital were written more from a genealogical perspective than from a historical one. My research resulted in a series of articles from 1975 to 1978 in the newspaper of Louisville, *The News and Farmer,* entitled "Those Glorious Days." To some extent, this book grew out of those articles, but it is much more extensive than that series.

This book studies the history of Louisville and Jefferson County mainly during the time that it was the capital of Georgia, from 1796 to 1807. Since it is important to set the scene for the coming of the capital to this area, however, the first chapter deals with the area around Louisville before the capital came there. It touches on the Indians of the area, the creation of Queensborough, the importance of George Galphin as a "frontier diplomat," and activities in this area immediately following the Revolutionary War. These items set the stage for the coming of the capital to Louisville.

The second chapter looks at Louisville the capital in terms of the governmental activities that took place there during this period. It covers such matters as the establishment of the capital and the construction of its buildings in Louisville, the creation of Jefferson County, the taxes of this period, the importance of militia groups, and other important events pertaining to the government while Louisville was Georgia's capital.

Chapter three contains studies of the daily life of Louisville during its capital period. Sections on safety, business actitity, professionals, printing and newspapers, entertainment, religious life, and education appear.

The final chapter looks at what happened to Louisville in the years immediately after the capital relocated to Milledgeville. It includes discussions on governmental life, taxes, business acitivity, printing and newspapers, professionals, and religious life.

The sources for this book are Georgia government records, Louisville city records, records of Jefferson County, early Louisville and Georgia newspapers, original manuscripts in the Georgia Department of Archives and History and many secondary sources. Major sources for chapters, two, three, and four were Louisville newspapers of that early era.

All of these sources point out the importance of Louisville and the tremendous impact that it had on the history of early Georgia. Thus, it is very surprising that a detailed history has not been written on this important city before. I hope that this book will now fill the void and will provide a better understanding of the importance of Louisville and of the significant time in history when it was the capital of the state of Georgia.

I must thank many people for their help in making this book possible. When I first began this project I received much encouragement and assistance from Kathryn Rowell, who was then a librarian at the Jefferson County library. West Georgia College, where I was employed at the time much of the research for this book was done, provided me with some financial assistance that enabled me to do much of the research. I must also express appreciation to Ronald Melton and Don Pace, both professors of history at Brewton-Parker College and Murray Ward, associate vice president for development at Brewton-Parker College, for their help in reading and evaluating this manuscript. Ms. Philippa Denny should be given a special word of thanks because of her continuous encouragement concerning this book and the many different types of assistance that she has given in making this book become a reality. I must likewise thank my wife, Elizabeth, for reading and giving constructive criticism on the manuscript, as well as encouraging me during the long process of research and writing and tolerating my many piles of research materials scattered all over our home. Particular thanks must be given to Margaret Oswalt, my personal secretary, without whose help I could not have finished this book. Her many hours of typing and deciphering my revisions made this book possible.

Yulssus Lynn Holmes
Brewton-Parker College
Mount Vernon, Georgia

1
Before the Coming of the Capital

After the Revolutionary War, Georgia had to make some important decisions about its future, including where to locate its capital. Following much discussion and disagreement, the Georgia legislature decided to build a new town called Louisville and, when the government buildings were completed, to make it Georgia's capital.

Before the coming of the capital to Louisville, much had happened to make such an action possible. The changes in Georgia's border with the Indians and the growth in the state's population were major factors in locating the capital at Louisville. The significance of these changes becomes apparent in a quick review of how the Indians related to the area around Louisville and how the evolution of the state brought this land into the control of Georgia and made it into a settled place that could become the capital.

The Indian Inhabitants of the Area

The Indians who were most important to the Louisville area were the Creeks. The Lower Creek tribe was a confederacy of smaller tribes that occupied the region stretching through central Georgia and across the Chattahoochee River into central Alabama. These were the Creeks who were maonly in possession of the land covered by the grant of the Georgia charter and who hunted and had claims on the land in and around Louisville and Jefferson County.[1]

The early Indian history of the Louisville area mainly centered around the site of Old Town. For the Indians some of the more sacred river sites became known as "old towns" or "old fields." Old Town, located on the Ogeechee River in Jefferson County, was such a place. In the late seventeenth and early eighteenth centuries Ogeechee Old Town and other nearby Indian sites were populated by Yuchees, a part of the Creek confederation.[2]

Following the Yamassee War between the Creeks and the British in 1715, most of the Indians in eastern and central Georgia relocated with the Creek tribes along the Chattahoochee River in an attempt to escape problems with the British who had settled along the Atlantic coast.[3] At this time Old Town was abandoned by the Indians and remained uninhabited until the early 1750s. Although they moved, the Creeks did not abandon their long-standing claim to the whole of southern and eastern Georgia.[4]

Settlers on the Ogeechee Frontier

The Georgia trustees originally hoped to create a colony of small compact settlements populated by small landowners who were ready to cultivate their farms industriously in peace and defend them valiantly in war. Their idea resulted in a slowly growing, poor colony with backward conditions that did not improve until the trustees lifted some restrictions and Georgia was allowed to become more like South Carolina.[5]

A small number of people seem to have settled along the Ogeechee River in the 1740s even though there were many restrictions against such settlements.[6] Beginning in the early 1750s, however, Georgia's governing authorities began to encourage "up-country" or "frontier" settlements with the promise of free land, although the Creeks had never officially ceded any land other than a small strip along the Georgia coast around the original Savannah settlement.[7] As a result, small farmers began migrating from the Carolinas and Virginia and the Georgia coast to as far west as the Ogeechee River near Louisville.

Clearly, settlers were moving into the Jefferson County area near Louisville as early as 1755. A petition from Edward Brown and thirty-seven other people on 13 January 1755 indicated that this group had come from several of the neighboring provinces to settle in Georgia and that they had found a quantity of uncultivated and vacant lands on the north side of the Great Ogeechee River about one hundred miles from its mouth. They had settled there, and they were applying for proper grants to this land. They also asked the governor and his council to take the necessary measures with the Indians "to secure them from their insults" since the Indians had made many threats against them and had brought fear to the group.[8] Andrew Lambert petitioned for 400 acres on the Great Ogeechee just below the site of Ogeechee Old Town in 1756.[9]

In September 1756 these and other frontier settlers almost caused a war with the Indians. A group of Georgia frontiersmen pursued a party of Creeks that they believed were horse thieves and killed three of them. In the days that followed, the settlers abandoned the area near the Ogeechee River and fled to Augusta.[10] Fortunately, before any other bad incidents occurred, an Upper Creek chief came to Savannah and Governor John Reynolds was able to negotiate a peace with him.[11]

Although the situation between the settlers and the Indians improved, Governor Reynolds received a petition on 12 April 1757 from some settlers on the Great Ogeechee River pointing out that they were under "extreme Hardship by the Indians destroying their Grain and Stock, and Stealing their Horses." They said that these problems had discouraged some new families from coming to settle in Georgia and had encouraged others to leave the area.[12]

These settlements along the Ogeechee River greatly angered the Indians, and their threat of retaliation in 1756 caused panic for months in Augusta and surrounding outposts, such as Old Town.[13] When the hysteria caused by fear of a possible massacre passed, the Georgia government moved quickly to improve relationships with the Indians. The resulting treaty of 1763 temporarily pacified the concerned Creeks and, more importantly, redefined the boundaries of Georgia.[14] By this treaty, signed at Augusta on 10 November 1763, the Creek Indians transferred the territory lying roughly southeast of Little River and between the Savannah and the Ogeechee rivers to the colony of Georgia. For the next twenty years the Ogeechee River and most of Jefferson County and the Louisville area formed a significant portion of the Georgia frontier with the Indians.

Greatly involved in this land cession was a Scotch-Irish immigrant named George Galphin, who was a successful Indian trader in Georgia and South Carolina. Governor James Wright of Georgia wrote Galphin and asked him to assist the Georgia government in obtaining this Indian land cession.[15] Knowing that the government leadership was to meet with the Indians in Augusta beginning on 3 November 1763, Galphin entertained the headmen of the Lower Creeks in his establishment at Silver Bluff, an Indian "old town" and former principal town of the Yuchee Indians located about twelve miles below Augusta on the South Carolina side of the Savannah River.[16] Galphin's hospitality put them in a cheerful frame of mind about the meeting and helped make the treaty possible.[17] Even though relations had now improved with the Indians, Georgia officials did not trust the Indians. Therfore, they asked George Galphin to go along with the surveyors when the boundary line was defined so that the Indians could not make any changes in it.[18] Louisville and much of Jefferson County were included in this particular land cession.

Immigrants now began to pour into the frontier areas of Georgia. A large number were from Virginia and North Carolina where the soil had become exhausted. They rode their ponies over the trails, brought their slaves, and "cracked" their whips. These "Crackers" as they were called, were not liked by Governor James Wright, and he considered them "a set of vagabonds often as bad or worse than the Indians themselves." These people probably furnished a large portion of the early citizens of the Louisville area.[19]

As soon as the fertile land between the Savannah and Ogeechee rivers became legally available for settlement, many colonists besieged the Georgia government with petitions for land grants in this area. George Galphin, who had assisted Governor James Wright with the 1763 Indian land cession, was one of those who applied for such land grants. In March 1764 Galphin secured a grant of 500 acres "on Great Ogeechee at the Ford near by Lambert's settlements," in what is now part of Jefferson County. Later he bought 1,000 acres from Lambert, including his original settlement on the Ogeechee River. Ogeechee Old Town was on this land.[20]

When the frontier officially moved from the Savannah River to the Ogeechee River, Galphin apparently realized the necessity of controlling the Yuchee Indian trail from his home at Silver Bluff to where it entered Indian territory at Old Town. This was necessary in order to ensure his control of trade with the Creeks at Coweta Town on the Chattahoochee River.[21] Even before Georgia governor James Wright signed Galphin's grant to Old Town in 1767,[22] this Scotch-Irish Indian trader had enlarged this settlement with a trading post and large cowpens. His trading post at Old Town supplied nearby families with manufactured goods and products as well as some staples that were necessary to make their lives more enjoyable.[23]

Queensborough

In February 1764 Governor James Wright obtained the passage of an act by the Georgia Assembly to encourage settlers to come to Georgia. Simply stated, this act provided land for any group of Protestant families exceeding forty people. These people were exempted from taxes with the exception of those with slaves.

Needless to say, this act attracted a great deal of attention from businessmen who saw it as an opportunity to enrich themselves as well as to help the colony of Georgia. A key person in this effort was George Galphin. In January of 1765, the governor and council of Georgia were petitioned by George Galphin, Lachlan McGillivray, and John Rea for fifty thousand acres of land to be laid out in one or more townships for settlers from Ireland. Their petition was granted and they received vacant land between the Ogeechee River, Briar Creek, Buck Head Creek, and the Lower Creek Path to set up an Irish township, contingent on it being settled in three years. This land was located in Jefferson County, just a few miles south of Louisville.[24]

It should be noted that the land George Galphin had already acquired around Old Town was about in the center of this proposed township, and he had been steadily acquiring more land between the Savannah and Ogeechee Rivers since 1750. John Rea also had a cowpen on Briar Creek and owned other land in the area.[25]

Having received permission from the Georgia government to begin the new township, Galphin and Rae now had to convince Irish Protestants to immigrate there.[26] They began to write to friends and relatives in that country during 1765 and 1766, and they advertized their new township in the *Belfast News-Letter*, which was the major newspaper of northern Ireland.

On 15 May 1765, John Rea wrote to his brother in Ireland and later his letter was printed in the *Belfast News-Letter*. In this letter he informed people that he had been given a grant for 50,000 acres of land in Georgia "for any of my friends and countrymen that have a mind to come to this country and bring their families here to settle." Rea told them that "the land I have chosen is very good for wheat and any kind of grain, indigo, flax, and hemp will grow to great perfection, and I do not know any place better situated for a flourishing township than this place will be."[27]

Shortly after the publication of Rea's letter, George Galphin also put some advertisement in the *Belfast News-Letter*. He stated that "each master of a family shall have a hundred (100) acres of good land and everyone that belongs to him shall have fifty (50) acres free from all taxes and quiet rent for the term of ten (10) years." When there were enough immigrants, he would send a ship to bring them over to Charleston and from thence they would have "free passage" in his own boat to their plantation."[28]

After two years of advertising and recruiting for their new township, Rea and Galphin had still not attracted any immigrants to Georgia. As a result, on 1 March 1768 they asked the Georgia Assembly for a one-year extension on their grant. They argued that the inducement given by South Carolina to immigrants had been extended to 1768 and had attracted all the potential settlers. With the end of the South Carolina Bounty Act, Rea and Galphin assured the Georgia Assembly that they could bring settlers to Georgia provided Georgia would pay the passage for those immigrants.[29]

With the approval for the renewed grant by the Georgia Assembly, Rea and Galphin began to work even harder on their settlement program. In June 1768, they arranged for a ship to be sent from Belfast to Savannah. They sent Matthew Rea, John Rea's brother, and a William Beatty throughout northern Ireland to recruit immigrants. At the end of 1768, the ship *Prince George* sailed towards Savannah with 107 immigrants on board.[30]

Governor Wright encountered numerous problems with this new settlement. The biggest of these was that the British board of trade, which was responsible for the colonies, decided against providing funds for the new settlement but was very slow in informing Governor Wright of its decision. In fact, when they did inform him, the settlers were already in Georgia. He solved this problem by taking money out of his own budget to help resettle the immigrants. When these settlers arrived, he was also faced with the problem of giving the township a name. He solved this problem quickly by coming up with the name Queensborough, after Queen Anne.[31]

To move these immigrants from Savannah to Queensborough, John Rea, in December of 1768, advertised for wagons to carry the women and children up to the new settlement. In February of 1769, thirty-nine of these immigrants and their families were granted 7,150 acres of land in the Queensborough township. Others of these immigrants also received grants at a later time.[32]

Each of the grantees was given a lot in the town of Queensborough, as well as a farming land grant of 100 to 150 acres. The idea of the settlement was like that of the French and English farming areas where the farmers lived in a village and held farm lands outside the village bounds. It is likely, however, that each settler built his log cabin on his own lot.[33]

No plat of the town of Queensborough has survived, but from descriptions of the boundaries of individual grants, it is clear that the intended site lay just west of Lambert's Big Creek, about three miles from the present town of Louisville.[34]

With the original approval for the township, the territory around Queensborough received some attention from land speculators who thought that this once deserted territory might become a good place to live or a place in which they might make some money. Many grants were made to people for land surrounding the Queensborough township and settlers steadily moved in.[35] In the belief that the development of the township would increase the value of land in the area, even leading citizens such as Governor Wright and James Habersham, president of the Georgia council, secured adjoining grants of 2,000 and 1,500 acres respectively along Rocky Comfort Creek in 1769. George Galphin and John Rea also increased the size and number of their cowpens in the area.

Because of the great success with all of the immigrants on the first ship, in July 1769 Matthew Rea began to advertise again for Irish immigrants. As a result of his work, the ship *Hopewell* left Belfast on 5 October 1769 with some 166 immigrants and arrived in Savannah on 6 December 1769.[36]

A few days after their arrival in Georgia, the *Hopewell* immigrants petitioned for assistance. They claimed that they had already spent all their money on travel and had nothing to help them settle in the new township. The Georgia Council provided 200 pounds to be paid to John Rea and his son-in-law Samuel Elbert to supply the needs of the *Hopewell* passengers until they could settle at Queensborough.[37]

In April the *Belfast News-Letter* published a letter from a disgruntled passenger on this ship with the heading "he who can't find bread in Ireland will not find it any where." The writer was one of those who, dissatisfied with what Georgia had to offer, had demanded a free passage to Charleston as Matthew Rea had promised.[38]

Possibly because of this adverse publicity, Matthew Rea was not very successful in finding immigrants in 1770. Rea advertized in June of 1770, but gathered only a few passengers for the ship *Hopewell*. This time forty-five passengers landed at Savannah, and in January of 1771, they obtained grants totaling 2,550 acres in Queensborough.[39]

On 4 February 1771, John Rea submitted a petition to the Georgia Council asking for a grant of 25,000 additional acres, claiming that all the "plantable" land of Queensborough had already been given to Irish settlers. His request was granted.[40]

In July 1771, Matthew Rea announced that the *Britannia* would sail for Savannah at the end of October. By the time it reached Savannah

with its immigrants an epidemic of smallpox and measles had broken out
on the ship, taking the lives of twenty-nine children. The ship and its
passengers were quarantined immediately. The minutes of the Georgia
Council indicate that only twenty-six of the families ever received grants,
totaling 5,200 acres in the Queensborough township.[41]

Because the township was so close to the border with the Indians,
there were always problems between the white and red people at Queensborough. In February 1770 the settlers around Queensborough were
complaining about trouble with the Indians, and they petitioned the
Georgia Assembly to build a fort in their area and to station scouts to
remove Indians who crossed the Ogeechee River. The Georgia authorities
did not respond to their request.[42]

In October 1771, a number of Queensborough settlers became exas-
perated by continual horse stealing and began to pursue the Indians that
they believed to be the thieves. The expedition crossed into Indian
territory and killed one Indian and severely beat another. The Georgia
authorities were very disturbed by this turn of events, and James Habersham, the president of the Georgia Council, immediately called on
George Galphin for assistance. Galphin was able to calm both the settlers
in Queensborough as well as the Indians, and peace was restored for a
few months.[43]

In early December 1771, a Queensborough resident by the name of
John Carey was killed by Creek Indians to whom he had given hospitality. Once again George Galphin was called into action. His influence
on the Indians was so strong that the Creeks took the unprecedented
action of putting the killer to death in the presence of several Indian
traders.[44]

No word of the perils to which the Queensborough settlers had been
exposed was allowed to reach Ireland, and in June 1772 Matthew Rea
was again advertising for immigrants. This was a year of heavy im-
migration, with some thirty immigrant ships sailing from ports in the
north of Ireland. At the beginning of July the *Britannia* again announced
for Charleston and Savannah. This ship reached Charleston on 11 January
1773, but there is no record of it having called at Savannah.[45]

Matthew Rea advertised the ship *Elizabeth* at the beginning of
August 1772, and it was supposed to sail with immigrants and a cargo of
beef and bread on 9 November. It was delayed several times before it
arrived in Savannah, and only two people on this ship can be identified
as having received grants of land at Queensborough.[46]

Events in Georgia during 1772 were leading to a crisis in Indian relations. Governor James Wright's hopes of further expansion had been raised by the offer of the Cherokees in December 1770 to give up land in payment of their debts to George Galphin and other Indian traders. By promising to distribute proceeds from future sales of this ceded land to the indebted traders, Governor Wright proposed to liquidate the Indians' debt.[47] He went to England in July 1772, where he worked hard to win the government's approval for this deal. The Queensborough and other frontier incidents were valuable evidence for the necessity of pushing the frontier farther back.[48] In December 1772 he returned to Georgia to put this agreement into effect. A treaty was signed at Augusta in June 1773 by which the Creeks and Cherokees ceded to Georgia more than two million acres lying north of the Little River and west of the Savannah River.[49]

The cession of land, however, had been mainly a Cherokee idea, with the Creeks strongly opposed to it. It only served to heighten Indian unrest in the Georgia backcountry, increasing Indian resentment against settlers coming to the Georgia frontier. A real crisis came on Christmas Day of 1773 and again in January of 1774, when parties of Lower Creek warriors attacked the Georgia frontier, killing thirteen settlers. Some militia groups who set out in pursuit of the Indians were repulsed on 23 January with the loss of several lives. This threw the frontier area, Queensborough in particular, into panic. As a result, both Indians and settlers threatened a full-scale war. Governor Wright reacted by closing down the Indian trade in Georgia.[50]

At this exact time, when the problems with the Indians were so numerous, the greatest exodus of immigrants from the north of Ireland to the American colonies occurred. Hearing news of the Indian problems, most potential Irish settlers were frightened away from Queensborough. Others who had already settled in Queensborough moved away.

The ship *Waddell* sailed for Georgia in November 1773, arriving at Savannah in late February 1774. The arrival of these passengers came at a bad time. Just a few days before its landing a group who had come out on the *Elizabeth* petitioned the Georgia Council telling of their trials at Queensborough. They claimed that many of the settlers from Queensborough Township had fled to North and South Carolina because of the Indian dangers. Thus the *Waddell* passengers quickly decided to settled in some place other than Queensborough. This was the last ship of immigrants from Ireland to reach Georgia before the Revolution, and this marked the end of the Queensborough settlement scheme by Galphin and Rea.[51]

One cannot be certain about how many people actually settled in this township. Information exists for tracing some 250 or so immigrants to Queensborough, but there are recorded grants for only 95 or 96 families. These grants amounted to no more than 20,000 acres of the 75,000 acres that were finally given to the township.[52]

The population of Queensborough was estimated in 1770 to be about 70 families, with 200 more families in the environs, who were "mostly Irish." Even though this was not a large number, it was a considerable addition to the small white population of the colony of Georgia.[53]

Unfortunately the town of Queensborough never really became a reality. There is little evidence that the town lots at Queensborough actually were occupied or developed into a real settlement. The only institution established in the settlement was a church. When the first settlers for Queensborough were being recruited in Ireland, they were advised by John Rea to bring with them a minister and a school master.[54] The Georgia government set aside fifty acres in Queensborough Township for a church and five hundred acres for a "Glebe."[55] Apparently this land was used for its intended purpose. The Queensborough settlers, who were mainly Presbyterians, had no desire for a clergyman of the Established Church of England and in 1773 expressly petitioned against the appointment of one for the lower part of St. George's Parish.[56]

Probably, the people of Queensborough erected a small log combination meeting house and school, but there is no evidence to prove it. A Presbyterian church was certainly established in the area, probably at Ebenezer or Bethel located near the modern town of Vidette, and Rev. Thomas Beattie became the first minister. He died two years after immigrating from Ireland.[57] The Reverend William Ronaldson was the next minister, and he created religious and political dissension in Queensborough during the American Revolution and was driven out of the community because of his Tory sympathies. He died at Charleston in 1783.[58] The Reverend David Bothwell also worked with the Queensborough community as well as the Bethel and Ebenezer churches when he arrived from Ireland in 1790.[59]

As the American Revolution began, some of the Queensborough settlers were Tories and aided the English soldiers. These loyalists lost their lands and stock at the end of the war. In a one-day sale in February 1782, no less than 2,650 acres of confiscated land were sold in

Queensborough.[60] In fact, the site of early Louisville was situated on land confiscated from David Russell, one of the original Queensborough settlers who came in 1768.[61]

There was much destruction and fighting around Queensborough during the Revolutionary War. According to letters from Lachlan McIntosh and Patrick Carr, the area around Queensborough and Old Town was the front line between the Americans and the British, and it changed hands numerous times. Most of the settlers were forced to flee from this area because of the British and Tory harassment.

Soon after the Revolutionary War, the Georgia legislature laid out plans for the new capital city of Louisville only a short distance away from Queensborough. With the establishment of Louisville, Queensborough soon lost its identity altogether and basically disappeared from the pages of history.

Galphin the Frontier Diplomat

During the fighting and destruction of the Revolutionary War, George Galphin acted as a backwoods diplomat on the Georgia frontier. He probably did more than anyone else to save the lives of settlers and Indians alike in the Georgia back country. He helped to keep the southern Indians neutral, and he prevented most of them from aiding the British in their attacks against the frontiers of Georgia.

In the spring of 1775, Galphin began to correspond with patriot leaders in Charleston and Savannah, and thereafter he accepted an increasingly prominent political role in the struggle against the British. Galphin himself had become very disenchanted with the way that the British were handling the Indians and Indian trade. A strained relationship with Governor Wright and the superintendent of Indian affairs, John Stuart, developed over these matters. John Stuart and David Taitt, the two main British Indian agents in the South, distrusted Galphin and did everything possible to discredit him in the eyes of the British government.[62]

Being aware of the growing inability of local patriot leaders to deal effectively with the deteriorating Indian-white relations in the backcountry, the Continental Congress of the new American government decided on a policy of neutrality toward the Indians and appointed the first committee on Indian affairs. They selected John Walker of Virginia and Willie Jones of North Carolina to serve as commissioners in the southern region and authorized the South Carolina Council of Safety to name three others to serve with them.

When the South Carolina Council met in Charleston on 2 October 1775, members wasted no time in choosing Edward Wilkinson, Robert Rae, and George Galphin to fill the remaining posts of commissioners of Indian affairs of the southern region.[63]

George Galphin was the most important of these Indian commissioners. He had lived for a long time among the Indians, and he knew and understood them well. Most of the Indians knew and appreciated him. Galphin also had several Indian mistresses and numerous half-Indian children. Long before the Revolutionary War, Galphin had proved his diplomatic ability through his frequent negotiations for the Indians, the British, and the Georgia government. He had a record that both the Indians and the frontier people of Georgia could respect.[64]

The commission Galphin received charged him with preserving "peace & friendship" with the Indians, and he apparently accepted the charge willingly. He developed a policy of "rum and good words," which kept the Georgia Indians peaceful for most of the Revolutionary War, causing great concern for the British. In fact, Galphin caused the British so much trouble that in 1778 they offered a reward of five hundred pounds sterling for him dead or alive.[65]

In the beginning of the war Galphin continued to invite the Indians to his home in Silver Bluff, but he promptly stopped this practice. Probably in order to keep the settlers and Indians as far apart as possible, he started entertaining and negotiating with the Indians at his trading post on the Ogeechee River at Old Town in Jefferson County. Galphin ran a type of "shuttle diplomacy" between the Ogeechee trading post and Silver Bluff with much of his time being spent away from home.[66]

Shortly after the signing of the Declaration of Independence Galphin learned of a massacre on the Ogeechee River. In order to prevent further hostilities, he rode immediately to Old Town and found out the details of the incident. Creek warriors, who felt they had never received satisfaction for the previous murder of a kinsman, had shot and smashed the head of one white settler. A long talk addressed to the Creek headmen apparently convinced them to restrain from further frontier raids for the time being.[67]

Galphin spent the fall of 1776 working frantically to prevent the settlers on the Georgia frontier from declaring war on the Creeks. On 26 October Galphin wrote of his dilemma to Willie Jones, a fellow Indian commissioner: "I have a hard task to keep the Creeks our friends, when both our enemies and the people that should be our friends want us to be at war with them." Galphin explained that he had been forced to send home Indians waiting to see him at Old Town because "some of the people upon the ceded land said they would come down and kill them," and, moreover, that "the people upon the ceded land . . . say they will kill them wherever they meet them."[68]

With the help of Henry Laurens, a key patriot leader as well as an important South Carolina merchant and planter, Galphin got permission from the Continental Congress to hold a major meeting with the Creeks. Due to the ever present danger of exposing Indians to backcountry settlers still desiring a Creek war, Galphin decided not to have the Indians come to Augusta or Silver Bluff but to meet them at Old Town on the Ogeechee River. Georgia governor John-Adam Treutlen attempted to ease tensions between Galphin and the settlers of the ceded lands before the Old Town meeting by issuing an official proclamation explaining the importance of this meeting for Georgia's security.[69]

Galphin and Rae welcomed almost 500 Creeks for this meeting in May of 1777.[70] Handsome Fellow from Okfuskee and representatives from other Upper towns attended, along with the Cusseta king and headmen from most of the Lower towns.[71] By holding these meetings at Ogeechee Old Town, the Indians could come from Indian territory to Galphin's meeting place by simply crossing the Ogeechee River and did not have to travel through any settler-controlled land.

Galphin began this meeting by expressing his regret that Creek blood had been spilled, and he asked them to continue to exercise restraint. He promised to send them goods if they drove British agents out of their towns. Galphin also extended an invitation from the Continental Congress for some of the headmen to visit Philadelphia.

In response to Galphin, the Indian leaders spoke of their desire to maintain peace and their immediate and pressing need for goods. The Philadelphia invitation did not appeal to them, but Handsome Fellow and eight other Creek leaders did go with Galphin to visit Charleston after the Old Town meeting.[72]

On their return from Charleston in early August this group came by Galphin's home at Silver Bluff and learned that there had been an Indian raid against the Georgia frontier in which Captain Thomas Dooly of the Third Georgia Continental Battalion and several other officers had been killed. Thomas Dooly's brother, Captain John Dooly of the Georgia Continental Regiment of Horse, rode to Silver Bluff and demanded that the Indians be detained until he received satisfaction for his brother's death. Galphin convinced Dooly to place the Indians in the custody of Robert Rae, who was not only a federal Indian commissioner but also a lieutenant colonel of the Second Georgia Continental Battalion. At the appropriate time, Rae released Handsome Fellow and his colleagues and helped them to return safely to Indian territory.[73]

Unknown to Galphin, Superintendent Stuart had developed a plan to assassinate him. In the summer of 1777, a party of Loyalists and Indians commanded by Lieutenant Samuel Moore of Florida agreed to carry out the murder. Moore's party penetrated into Georgia early in the summer and waited in the vicinity of Silver Bluff for an opportunity to strike. This opportunity presented itself on the day that Handsome Fellow and the other Creek chiefs left Silver Bluff for their return to the Ogeechee River. Thinking that Galphin would be accompanying the Indians, Moore's party ambushed them and killed Captain John Gerard, one of the Indians' escorts, whom the murderers apparently mistook for Galphin.[74] Galphin had remained at Silver Bluff and was thereby saved, but his close brush with death and the events related to it undoubtedly unnerved him and caused him to be pessimistic about future Creek neutrality.

Galphin knew quite well that pro-British factions controlled many Creek towns and that he must try to strengthen his position with the neutralist factions. He accordingly sent invitations to all the Creek headmen requesting that they meet him again at Old Town in November to conclude a "treaty of peace." The White Lieutenant of Okfuskee and Opeitley Mico of Tallassee agreed to attend as representatives from the Upper Creek towns, but headmen from ten other Upper towns and several Lower Creek towns not only refused to come but rather chose to visit Superintendent Stuart in British-controlled Pensacola. On 6 November 1777, about 350 Indians began meeting with Galphin at Old Town, and their meetings continued for seven weeks.

Because of the animosity of the frontier settlers against the Indians and the problems that had been experienced following the summer meetings at Old Town, Galphin made sure that proper measures were taken to maintain security. Continental troops escorted him and Robert Rae to Old Town and remained on guard throughout the period of negotiations so that the Indians attending the treaty would have full protection.[75]

At the beginning of the meeting, Galphin thanked the Indians for pushing the British out, and he asked that they not allow them to return.

He reminded them of the destruction that the Cherokees had experienced at the hands of the patriots and said that such things could happen to them if they allowed the British to come back.[76]

As the meeting ended, Galphin outfitted one hundred pack horses with goods, rum, and ammunition for the Indians to carry back with them to their respective towns. He also agreed to keep his trading post at Old Town well stocked so that all Creeks could visit and be supplied from there.[77]

During the spring of 1778 George Galphin spent all of his time at Ogeechee Old Town receiving Creek visitors, giving out gifts to the Indians and collecting information from them. Even as late as August 1778, Galphin was at Ogeechee Old Town.[78] He expressed only optimism about the situation in a letter to Henry Laurens in which he pointed out that hundreds of Creeks continued to trade with him at Old Town. In Galphin's words, "I have been nine weeks at Ogeechee upon the line and was not one day clear of Indians all the time I was there. I am but just come home and must go back in a day or two."[79]

Galphin's reception of Indian delegations at Old Town proved to be extremely effective as a way of sustaining anti-British sentiments among some of the Creek towns. The traditional neutralist faction among the Okfuskee and Cusseta continued to resist British demands that they sever all ties with Galphin.[80]

In July of 1778 several Creek bands set out for the Georgia frontier, where they burned cabins, slaughtered cattle and hogs, killed several dozen settlers, and captured one fort.[81] This raiding stopped when the Creek neutralists faction received word from Galphin that Georgia leaders, reacting to these vicious Creek raids, had forced him to stop all of his trading with the Indians.[82]

Galphin was very aware of the danger of not supplying the neutralists Indians with goods. As he explained in a letter to Henry Laurens, he had not been in favor of the trade embargo, but "the people upon the frontiers threatened to kill me & the Indians too if I supplied them." Galphin also placed all the blame for the raids during the summer of 1778 on the backcountry settlers of Georgia.[83]

At the same time that Galphin was explaining to Henry Laurens why the trade embargo was counterproductive, the Creek neutralists decided to meet with Galphin about their increasingly impoverished situation. They sent word to him of their desire to see him, and he agreed to meet them at Old Town. In December, 1778 Galphin received a group of

Indians at his place on the Ogeechee River. Among those present were Opeitley Mico, the Tallassee chief, the Cusseta king, and seven other Creek headmen. They came to beg for supplies, but Galphin could only promise the possibility of future supplies. At this meeting he talked about a "great peace meeting" to be held in the spring of 1779, but the inflamed condition of the frontier gave him little hope that it would ever take place.[84]

Unfortunately the peace meeting did not happen, but Galphin did manage to reopen the Old Town trading post in January of 1779 to supply some goods to the neutral Indians. Early in that month he wrote General Benjamin Lincoln that he "expected a good many Indians down at Ogeechee the last of this month to purchase goods." The optimistic tone of this letter indicates that Galphin hoped a renewal of Indian trading at Old Town might strengthen the neutralist faction. He could not foresee, however, that by the end of January not only would travel to Old Town be impossible, but that even his work as a federal Indian commissioner would be extremely difficult.[85]

At Old Town George Galphin worked hard for some four years to keep the Creek Indians neutral and to prevent a large-scale Indian war on the Georgia frontier. He provided the Indians with provisions from Old Town, held meetings with them there, and sent messages to them from there. But, alas, all of his efforts proved to be in vain once the British captured Savannah on 29 December 1778.

After taking Savannah, the British consolidated their power and gradually moved into the interior of Georgia to destroy rebel strongholds. They were particularly concerned about taking Augusta, Silver Bluff, and Ogeechee Old Town. During the winter of 1779, their assaults began with a force led by Archibald Campbell taking Old Town. George Galphin was forced to flee from Old Town and to abandon any further attempts at keeping the Indians neutral.[86] By 18 March 1779, affairs were in great distress even around Silver Bluff, and Galphin wrote to Henry Laurens telling about all his problems with marauding bands of British who caused his slaves to flee, drove off his horses, and killed his cattle. This situation got so bad that Galphin had to flee Silver Bluff during the night in order to escape capture. Yet, in the midst of all his problems, Galphin took time to send a message through to the one hundred Creeks who were on their way to meet him at Old Town in late January so that they would not expose themselves to danger.[87]

In the spring of 1779, David Taitt led about four hundred Creek warriors and fifty Loyalists to the Ogeechee River, where they burned several forts and also raided Old Town.[88] According to Daniel Mc-Murphy, who then lived at Old Town and worked in the trading post, this group carried off more than 1,400 pounds of skins and 14,000 pounds of flour.[89] Taitt's group, however, was prevented from joining Campbell's forces, and this caused the two British groups to withdraw from the Augusta area toward Savannah.[90]

Thereafter Continental forces exercised uncontested control over the Georgia backcountry for almost a year. During that time Galphin made some efforts to maintain contact with a few Creek towns, but the increasing number of confrontations between Creeks and whites along the frontier soon made communication almost impossible. Moreover, the raids on Silver Bluff and Old Town had taken all his supplies so he had no more to distribute. As a result, the entire Creek neutralist faction gave in to the pro-British faction and agreed to fight against their former patriot friends.[91]

In May of 1780, Thomas Brown, a Tory leader, led a force from Savannah to reoccupy Augusta and the Georgia frontier along the Ogeechee River. As a part of his campaign he captured Silver Bluff, constructed a fort there, and also arrested George Galphin. Brown charged the aging patriot commissioner with high treason and seemingly sent him to Savannah for trial.[92] Apparently the British dropped the charges against Galphin and allowed him to return to Silver Bluff, but he no longer took an active role in Indian affairs in Georgia or South Carolina. The British seizure of his frontier plantation and many other setbacks suffered by the patriots probably contributed to Galphin's death on 1 December 1780 at Silver Bluff.[93]

If Galphin had lived another year, he would have witnessed the reversal of the British military advantage in Georgia and South Carolina. In the late spring of 1781 a dramatic British retreat began. In May, Continental troops under the command of Lieutenant Colonel Henry Lee recaptured Silver Bluff and cut British supply lines altogether.[94] Elijah Clark and his militiamen launched an attack on Augusta in June, and Thomas Brown and his forces were forced to surrender.[95] Patrick Carr, in a letter from Silver Bluff in 11 August 1782, said, "Mr. Galphin's Settlement at the Old Town still stands by my persuasion."[96]

After the Revolutionary War

George Galphin was now gone and could not play a role in the peace talks that would come after the war. Old Town, however, was still in the memory of the Indians and the patriots, so when peace talks were considered with the Creeks, the first place the patriots thought of holding them was at Old Town. In 1782 a message was sent to the Indians concerning a treaty that was to be signed at "Old Town on Ogeechee" on 1 May 1782. It is not clear what happened at Old Town, but the records indicate that a treaty was actually signed between the Indians and Georgia patriots at Long Swamp in Jefferson County on 17 October 1782.[97]

The penalty for choosing the losing side was all too obvious to the Creeks. Georgia, like her sister states, looked upon Indian land as the spoils of war. The Georgia Assembly began calling for a conference with the Creeks as early as April of 1783 so that the Indian leaders could cede to Georgia all the land between the Ogeechee and Oconee Rivers as reparations "for the many injuries done that virtuous State."[98]

On 1 November 1783, Creek headmen met newly appointed Georgia commissioners in Augusta to cede their lands and make their peace with the Americans. This land cession moved the old frontier west to the Oconee River and added another section to Jefferson County.[99]

After this the situation did get better, as can be seen in a letter that Patrick Carr sent to Governor Hall from Old Town on the Ogeechee River on 10 December 1783. He talked about the improved situation on the Georgia frontier, telling the Georgia governor, Lyman Hall, that he had "lived on the frontiers for more than seven months" but there had been only "two horses stolen in that time within twenty miles of me, either by Indians or by Tories, and those two have been restored, for those rogues are afraid to come into this settlement."[100]

Shortly after the 1783 Indian treaty, the Galphin brothers, George and John, sons of George Galphin and the Creek princess Metawney, moved from Old Town to a 15,000-acre tract that the Georgia government had given them in Washington County on the Ogeechee's west bank, which is upstream from present-day Louisville. There they founded a village called "Galphinton."[101]

One should note that there was an "old" and a "new" Galphinton. The "old" Galphinton was at Old Town near Queensborough, and the "new" Galphinton was in Washington County. In the *Jefferson County*

Tax Digest of 1799, it mentions that one Francis Brown had two lots in "New Galphinton" in Washington County. The Governor's Letter Book of 21 June 1785 noted that a meeting was to have been held in "Galphinton, a few miles above the Old Town on Great Ogeechee." The *Gazette of the State of Georgia* in 1785 stated that a treaty with the Creek Indians would take place at Galphinton "on the south side of Ogeechee, about 20 miles above the Old Town." The "old" Galphinton was about ten miles south of Louisville on the Ogeechee River at the site of Old Town.[102]

It was at "new" Galphinton that the American commissioners came to deal with the Creek Indians on 12 November 1785. After two weeks of waiting, Indians from only two towns had come. The commissioners refused to negotiate with so few Indians, so they explained the purpose of the meeting, distributed presents, and left to meet the Cherokees at another place.[103]

The treaty of 1783 supposedly ended Indian-White conflict on the Georgia frontier, but in reality problems continued along the Ogeechee River until about 1790 and afterward along the Oconee River for many years to come. Even though peace treaties were signed with the Indians, there were Indian raids in the Jefferson County area as late as 1788. One group of four Indians came into Williamson Swamp and gave chase to four men and a boy, shooting and scalping one of them. This same group apparently came to a Mr. Crawford's plantation and set fire to his house and burned it and about one hundred bushels of corn.[104] Solomon Wood of "Woods Fort on Williamson Swamp, six miles from Old Town" on 14 March 1788 sent a petition concerning this matter to the Georgia governor.[105]

Georgia faced a tremendous problem of reconstruction after the Revolution. Many of her ablest men had left or been banished as loyalists. Plantations had been ravaged, buildings burned, and slaves stolen or absconded. Organized religion scarcely existed and morality had suffered as usual in wartime. Gambling, drunkenness, profanity, and violation of the Lord's Day were all too common. Churches and schools were in ruins, and the officials charged with restoring them neglected their duty. Additionally, Queensborough had quietly died, and Old Town had lost its importance as a trading and diplomatic center.

Many changes had come about as a result of the Revolutionary War. Clearly, however, better days were ahead for Georgia, because the state was steadily gaining in population and there was plenty of good land to be had.[106] As the state grew and made progress, it was also time for Georgia to give serious consideration to the location of its capital and to the potential "glorious days" that lay ahead for it.

Notes

[1]John P. Corry, *Indian Affairs in Georgia 1732–1756* (Philadelphia, 1936) 34, 69.

[2]Verner W. Crane, *The Southern Frontier 1670–1732* (Ann Arbor: University of Michigan Press, 1956) 36, 134.   [3]Ibid., 183.

[4]Louis Devorsey, Jr., *Indian Boundaries in the Southern Colonies. 1763–1775* (Chapel Hill: University of North Carolina Press, 1966) 64.

[5]Corry, *Indian Affairs*, 25.

[6]Allen D. Candler and Lucian Lamar Knight, eds.,*Colonial Records of the State of Georgia* (Atlanta, 1904–1916) 31:118. Hereafter *Colonial Records of the State of Georgia* will be abbreviated as *CRG*.

[7]Ibid., 7:398-400.   [8]Ibid., 7:93.   [9]Ibid., 9:141-42, 146-47.

[10]Ibid., 7:360, 390, 392, 395, 396, 399; 9:348, 668.

[11]Corry, *Indian Affairs*, 141 and *CRG*, 7:392-425.

[12]*CRG*, 7:537.   [13]Ibid., 7:390-97.

[14]Louis Devorsey, Jr., "Indian Boundaries in Colonial Georgia," *Georgia Historical Quarterly* 15/1 (Spring, 1970): 71-74.

[15]John H. Goff "Short Studies of Georgia Place Names, No. 78" *Georgia Mineral Newsletter* (Fall 1954): 129-36.

[16]Robert L. Meriwether, *The Expansion of South Carolina, 1729–1765* (Kingsport TN: Southern Publishers Inc., 1940) 69-70.

[17]David H. Corkran, *The Creek Frontier, 1540–1783* (Norman OK: University of Oklahoma Press, 1967) 238-39.

[18]*CRG*, 10:303.   [19]Ibid., 14:475-76.   [20]Ibid., 9:420-21.

[21]Lucien Lamar Knight, *Georgia's Landmarks Memorials and Legends* (Atlanta: Byrd Printing Company, 1914) 906; Letter of Hamilton Raiford, *News and Farmer* (Louisville), 25 July 1872.

[22]Pat Bryant, ed., *English Crown Grants in St. George Parish in Georgia, 1755–1775* (Atlanta: State printing Office, 1975), Grant Book E, 284, granted on March 3, 1767; Friedrick Peter Hamer, "Indian Traders, Land and Power— Comparative Study of George Galphin on the Southern Frontier and Three Northern Traders," (Masters thesis, University of South Carolina, 1982).

[23]Silver Bluff ledgers, Georgia Historical Society; *CRG*, 9:348, 414-15, 723; 10:706; 11:73.

[24]*CRG*, 7:873, 697; 9:269, 14:348; 17:263; 23:39-40: Loris D. Cofer, *Queensborough or the Irish Town and Its Citizens*, (by author, 1977).

[25]Ibid., 6:331.

[26]James G. Leyburn, *The Scotch-Irish: A Social History* (Chapel Hill: University of North Carolina Press, 1962) 169-75.

[27]*Belfast News-Letter* (Ireland), 3 September–22 October 1765. Hereafter the *Belfast News-Letter* will be abbreviated to *BNL*.

[28]Ibid., 4 March 1766.   [29]*CRG* 10:435.

[30]Advertisements for this ship appeared in the *BNL* 18 times between 26 July and 23 September 1768; *Georgia Gazette* (Savannah), 7 and 21 Dec 1768.

[31]Shelburne to Wright, 8 October 1767, in the Public Record Office, Colonial Office Papers, Ser. 5, vol. 676, fol. 9 and Wright to Lord Hillsborough, November 18, 1768, Ser. 5, vol. 660, fol. 25 and to the Board of Trade, 10 February 1769, Ser. 5, vol. 650, fol. 251-2; *CRG*, 10:671; 28:2:590; Knight, *Georgia Landmarks*, 701. Hereafter "in the Public Record Office, Colonial Office Papers" will be abbreviated C. O.

[32]*Georgia Gazette* (Savannah), 21 December 1768; *CRG* 10:696-98.

[33]Writings of John Cain in the Louisville Library.

[34]*CRG*, 10:706, 788, 828, 927.   [35]*CRG* 9:516; 10:194-95, 563, 788.

[36]There were 25 advertisements for this ship in the *BNL* between 7 July and 22 September 1769.   [37]*CRG* 15:81.

[38]*BNL*, 24 October 1769 and 27 April 1770; *South Carolina Gazette* (Charleston), 28 December 1769.

[39]Ibid., 5–22 June 1770; *South Carolina Gazette*, 10 January 1771; *CRG*, 11:227, 234, 273; 15:271-72.   [40]*CRG*, 12:212-13, 253.

[41]James Habersham to the Earl of Hillsborough, 31 October 1771, C. O., Ser. 5, vol. 661, fol. 214; *CRG*, 12:212-13, 253.   [42]*CRG*, 15:109-10.

[43]Ibid., 12:148-49; Habersham to Hillsborough, 31 October, 27 November, 1771, C. O., Ser. 5, vol. 661, fol. 167-82, 189.

[44]Habersham to Hillsborough, 30 Dec. 1771, 24 April 1772, C. O., Ser. 5, vol. 661, fol. 221-22, 229; *CRG* 12:150-54, 316-18, 17:657-60.

[45]*BNL*, 23 June–7 July 1772 and 3 July, 3–14 Aug 1772; *South Carolina Gazette*, 14 January 1773.

[46]*BNL*, 14 August–15 September 1772, 6–23 October 1772, 10 November 1772.   [47]C. O., Ser. 5, vol. 661, 327-72.

[48]To Hillsborough, 27 November 1771, C. O., Ser. 5, vol. 661, fol., 190.

[49]Walter H. Mohr, *Federal Indian Relations, 1774–1788* (Philadelphia: University of Pennsylvania Press, 1933) 14; DeVorsey, "Indian Boundaries," 76.

[50]John R. Alden, *John Stuart and the Southern Frontier: A Study of the Indian Relations, War, Trade, and Land Problems in the Southern Wilderness, 1754–1775* (Ann Arbor: University of Michigan Press, 1944) 301-12; David Taitt to John Stuart, 18 July 1774, C. O., Ser. 5, vol. 75.

[51]"Queensborough," *The Georgia Genealogist* 8 (Summer 1971): 4.

[52]E. R. R. Green, "Queensborough Township: Scotch-Irish Emigration and the Expansion of Georgia, 1763–1776," *William and Mary Quarterly*, 17/3rd series (April 1960): 198-99.

[53]John Gerard William DeBrahm. *History of the Province of Georgia* (Wormsloe, 1849) 4, 25; Green, "Queensborough Township," 198-99.

[54]*BNL*, 3 Sept 1765.   [55]*CRG*, 17:197.   [56]Ibid., 15:473.

[57]*Georgia Gazette*, 10 August 1774.

[58]David Stewart, *The Seceders in Ireland* (Belfast, 1950) 327, 335, 346. For Rev. Ronaldson, see also George Howe, *History of the Presbyterian Church in South Carolina* (Columbia SC, 1870) 643.

[59]George White, *Historical Collections of Georgia* (New York, 1854) 503-504; Emily Farmer, "Early Religious Life in Jefferson County." This is an unprinted article in the Jefferson County Library.

[60]Allen D. Candler, ed. *Revolutionary Records of Georgia* (Atlanta, 1908) 1:524-44.

[61]L. Q. C. Lamar, *A Compilation of the Laws of the State of Georgia, 1810–1819* (Augusta, 1821) 971.

[62]David Taitt to John Stuart, 17 December 1774, C. O., Ser. 5, vol. 76, fol. 37-38.

[63]*South Carolina Historical and Genealogical Magazine.* 2:99-100.

[64]Robert W.Gibbes, ed. *Documentary History of the American revolution, 1764–1782* (Spartanburg SC: The Reprint Company, 1972) 1: 159-69.

[65]James H. O'Donnel, III, *Southern Indians in the American Revolution* (Knoxville: University of Tennessee Press, 1973) 52, 69; Taitt to Stuart, 7 April 1778, C. O., Ser. 5 , vol. 79, fol. 152; George Galphin to Henry Laurens, 25 June 1778, Henry Laurens Papers, Sims Collection, South Carolinian Library, University of South Carolina, Columbia.

[66]Homer Bast, "Creek Indian Affairs, 1775–1778," *Georgia Historical Quarterly* 33/1 (1949): 1-25.

[67]Galphin to Willie Jones, 26 October 1776, in Peter Force, ed., *American Archives, Fifth Series* (Washington, 1837–1853) 3:648-50; Corkran, *The Creek Frontier*, 298.

[68]James H. O'Donnell, III, "Southern Indians in the War for American Independence, 1775–1783," in Charles M. Hudson, *Four Centuries of Southern Indians* (Athens: University of Georgia Press, 1975) 49; George Galphin to Willie Jones, 26 Oct 1776, in *American Archives*, 3:648-50.

[69]*CRG*, 1:311.   [70]Corkran, *The Creek Frontier*, 305.

[71]George Galphin to Henry Laurens, 20 July 1777, in the Henry Laurens Papers.   [72]Corkran, *The Creek Frontier*, 305-306.

[73]Robert Scott Davis, Jr., "George Galphin and the Creek Congress of 1777," *Proceedings and Papers of the Georgia Association of Historians* (1982): 21, 22.

[74]Ibid., 18-22. Also, John Stuart to William Knox, 26 August 1777, C. O., Ser. 5, vol. 78, fol. 220-21.

[75]*South Carolina and American General Gazette* (Charleston), 1 January 1778; "Order Book of Samuel Elbert," *Collections of the Georgia Historical Society*, 5:2:67-68.

[76]Indian Treaty of 6 November 1777, Laurens Papers.

[77]Corkran, *The Creek Frontier*, 310. Also, *South Carolina and American General Gazette*, 1 January 1778. [78]C. O. Ser. 5, vol. 78, fol. 117.

[79]George Galphin to Henry Laurens, 25 June 1778, Laurens Papers.

[80]Alexander McGillivray to John Stuart, 26 August 1778, C. O. Ser. 5, vol. 79, fol. 387. [81]C. O., Ser. 5, vol. 80, fol. 67 and 93.

[82]Corkran, *The Creek Frontier*, 317.

[83]George Galphin to Henry Laurens, 4 November 1778, Laurens Papers.

[84]Timothy Barnard to John Stuart, 9 November 1778, C. O., Ser. 5, vol. 80, fol. 101.

[85]George Galphin to Benjamin Lincoln, January 1779, in Galphin Papers, Newberry Library, Chicago; John McKay Sheftall, "George Galphin and Indian-White Relations in the Georgia Backcountry during the American Revolution," (Masters thesis, University of Virginia, 1980) 50.

[86]Diary of Archibald Campbell, 1779, photocopy in the Georgia State Library, Atlanta; O'Donnell, *Southern Indians*, 53-55.

[87]George Galphin to Henry Laurens, 18 March 1779, Laurens Papers.

[88]O'Donnell, *Southern Indians*, 53-55.

[89]Daniel McMurphy Affidavit, 12 February 1779, in File Two—McMurphy, Georgia Department of Archives and History, Atlanta.

[90]Gary D. Olson, "Thomas Brown, Loyalist Partisan, and the Revolutionary War in Georgia, 1777–1782, Part II," *Georgia Historical Quarterly* 54/2 (Summer 1970): 184.

[91]Florida Board of Commissioners to George Germain, 10 May 1779, C. O., Ser. 5, vol. 80, fol. 375. [92]*CRG* 15:590-91.

[93]Galphin Family Bible, photocopy in the Galphin Genealogical File, Georgia Department of Archives and History, Atlanta.

[94]Heard Robertson, "Second British Occupation of Augusta, 1780–1781," *Georgia Historical Quarterly* 58 (Winter 1974): 441; *CRG*, 12: 400.

[95]Martha C. Searcy, "1779: The First Year of the British Occupation of Georgia," *Georgia Historical Quarterly* 67/2 (Summer 1983): 169-88.

[96]"Letters of Partick Carr," *Georgia Historical Quarterly* 1 (1917): 337-38.

[97]MSS in the Georgia Department of Archives and History.

[98]Alexander McGillivray to Thomas Brown, 10 April 1783, C. O., Ser. 5, vol. 82, fol. 374. [99]*CRG*, 36:503-504.

[100]Partick Carr to Governor Hall, Old Town, 10 December 1783, in the Joseph V. Bevan Collection, of the Georgia Historical Society.

[101]*Revolutionary Records of Georgia*, 3:543; *Gazette of the State of Georgia*, 9 Mar 1786.

[102]*Columbian Museum and Savannah Advertiser* (Savannah), 15 January 1802; *Jefferson County Tax Digest*, 1799; Governor's Letter Book, 21, 23 June 1785, ; *Gazette of the State of Georgia* 29 Sept 1785.

[103]Kenneth Coleman *The American Revolution in Georgia 1763–1789* (Athens: University of Georgia Press, 1958) 243.

[104]*Georgia State Gazette*, 15 March 1788.

[105]Document in File II, Solomon Wood (Pre1800) in the Georgia Department of Archives and History.

[106]Reba Carolyn Strickland, *Religion and the State in Georgia in the Eighteenth Century* (New York: Columbia University Press, 1939) 161.

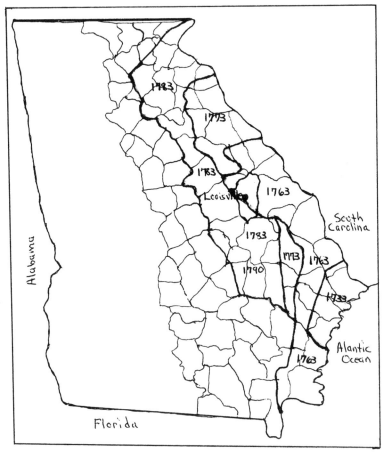

Georgia Indian Land Cessions of 1733, 1763, 1773, 1783, and 1790

2
Governmental Life in the Capital

The Making of a New Capital

When Georgia was a British colony, Savannah functioned as the colonial capital, although it was not officially designated as such. When Georgia became independent in 1776, the seat of government remained in Savannah. In December 1778, however, Savannah was captured by the British, and from then until January 1784, the Georgia legislature met at Augusta, with the exception of two terms, one of which convened at Herds Fort in Wilkes County and the other at Ebenezer in Effingham County. When the Revolutionary War ended, the legislature began meeting again in Savannah, but the people in upper Georgia had become quite happy with the convenience of having the capital located in Augusta. Thus many "up-country" people began to complain about having to make the long, expensive and dangerous journey from their homes all the way to Savannah.[1] At this time the desirability of transferring the seat of government to some point further inland became a topic of great discussion and dispute.[2]

A good example of this dispute is a letter of Isaac Briggs, a Georgian of some note and standing, which he wrote to a friend in Philadelphia on 6 March 1786. Briggs wrote:

> With us the point disputed at present is where the seat of the Government shall be? It has hitherto been at Savannah, but that being at one corner of the state and the place most thickly settled being at the distance of near 200 miles from Savannah, the Upper Country people, as they are called, having a majority in the house of Assembly have decreed that the seat of the government shall be at Galphinton about hundred miles from Savannah, and the lower Country People are displeased at having the seat of the Government removed from the place where it has always been held.[3]

Although there was some heated rivalry between the people that lived on Georgia's coastal areas and the people that lived inland, the major reason behind the move to relocate the capital was the fact that the population had moved northward, and Savannah was far from the most heavily populated and developing areas of Georgia. With the addition of new land acquired from the Indians, this population shift became even greater. Realizing this, the people on the frontier areas, as well as the people living in Savannah, decided that the capital should not be located in Augusta on the border of South Carolina but rather in some better situated place.

On 26 January 1786, the legislature of Georgia met in Augusta and passed a law that appointed Nathan Brownson, William Few, and Hugh Lawson as commissioners. They were to

> proceed and fix on a place, which they may think most proper and convenient, for erecting of public buildings, and establishing a seat of government and the university; provided the same shall be within twenty miles of Galphin's old town." They were also given the power to purchase a tract of land for that purpose, which should "not exceed one thousand acres, and to lay out a part thereof in lots, streets, and alleys, which shall be known by the name of Louisville.[4]

The Louisville commissioners were authorized to bargain and sell, to accept securities for payment, and to issue legally binding titles so that they could fully carry out their duties. They were required to give bond and security to the governor of the state in the amount of £6,000, and they were to receive compensation for their expenses provided they did not "exceed two dollars each day."[5]

In order to obtain the necessary funds for the acquisition of the Louisville site and to build the new capital, the commissioners were authorized to sell the government house and lot in Savannah. Any monies coming from this source and the revenues received from the sale of public lots in Louisville were to be applied to the erection of the public buildings in Louisville.[6] In 1789, Hugh Lawson and John Shelman, who were commissioners of Louisville, put an advertisement in the *Augusta Chronicle and Gazette of the State* saying: "We do hereby inform the public, that we will sell lots in Louisville by private sale."[7]

Even with this official beginning of Louisville in 1786, one should not think that the capital would move there quickly. A site had to be chosen for this new town, land had to be acquired, and buildings had to be built. Because of these things, Augusta was to continue as the temporary capital of the state and all of the state offices were to be located there until the new capital was completed.[8]

The commissioners chose a site for the new seat of government on the south side of Rocky Comfort Creek where it runs into the Ogeechee

River. Here the Georgia government had confiscated a thousand acres from the Tory David Russell after the Revolutionary War. Roger Lawson had purchased this land, and he was willing to sell it to the Louisville commissioners. The fact that one of the commissioners was his son, Hugh Lawson, certainly helped to make this land transaction possible.[9]

Louisville was to begin as a "ready-made" town, a town laid out with streets and buildings but without population. The new city was named for King Louis XVI of France because of all the help that France had given to the American colonies during the Revolutionary War.[10] The state house was to be near the center of the town, with broad streets running north and south that were named after trees and east and west streets that were named numerically. The town was laid out in a square with streets placed in right angles in the same pattern as the city of Philadelphia. There were to be eleven streets, with First Street bordering on the Ogeechee River and Rocky Comfort Creek, and with the state house on Sixth Street.[11]

Even after the site had been selected and the plans of the city had been designed, there was little activity in building the new Georgia capital. The demoralized condition of the state following the Revolutionary War was certainly one of the chief causes for the delay in building the new capital.[12] Indian problems also prevented early construction. The treaty made with the Creeks at Galphinton in 1785 was broken by them, and until 1796 an intermittent war with the Indians raged on the Georgia frontier. Louisville was really a frontier settlement, and everything to the west of it was basically uninhabited forest and Indian hunting land.[13] Other causes also hindered the completion of the new capital, including a lack of sufficient funds and the death during construction, of the state-house contractor.

Even with all of these problems, the commissioners of Louisville moved as quickly as they could to get the new capital built. In the *Georgia State Gazette* of 21 April 1787, they placed the following announcement:

> To be let by the commissioners of Lewisville to the lowest bidder the making of 100,000 well sized merchantable bricks for the public buildings to be delivered in government's square. There is clay, wood, and water on the public land. Any person inclined to undertake will please send their proposals sealed up to Hugh Lawson at Lewisville on or before the first day of June next at which time such proposals will be opened and the lowest terms accepted on the parties giving security for the performance. One half of the money will be paid on the brick

being kilned, the other half to be paid on the brick being delivered. The bricks to be delivered within three months from the time of undertaking.[14]

As construction began, there were concerns about the cost of this project. In a report of 11 December 1792, the House of Representatives showed its unhappiness with the progress of the new capital and made certain changes. The representatives thought that some of the charges were too high, so they appointed Thomas Shields, Abraham Jones, and William Little as commissioners "to examine what some ought in justice to be deducted from the several charges exhibited in the accounts of said commissioners."[15]

The sum of £200 was to be appropriated for the year 1793 for the purpose of completing the public buildings in Louisville. This money was to be paid into the hands of Robert Forsyth, James Jones, and John Twiggs, who were appointed as "sole commissioners to carry on the said buildings." It was their job to let the buildings to the lowest bidder and be obliged to have "the same completed within three years from the date hereof, agreeable to the original plan which they shall in no wise alter." Although the state wanted the public buildings at Louisville completed as soon as possible, many people recognized that things might move more slowly than desired because "the situation of the state at present harassed by Indians on the frontier and distressed by failure of crops is such as to be improper to appropriate a fund during the present session for that purpose."[16]

Of all the public buildings that were being built in Louisville, the most important and most controversial was the state house. This building was started at one point, and then the contractor died and was unable to finish the structure. The state was then forced to put the state house up for bids again. It is also clear that there were financial problems with the building. In an act passed on 20 December 1792 the commissioners of Louisville were authorized and empowered to purchase confiscated property up to £2,000-worth, "for the purpose of carrying on and completing the state house of Louisville, on the same term as the commissioners of the academies of the respective counties."[17]

In the *Augusta Chronicle and Gazette of the State* of 24 August 1793, the state announced that bids would be let on the state house. They gave a general description of what the structure was to be like:

The building is to be of brick, sixty feet long, forty wide and thirty-two feet high with the middle wall, and to be finished as soon as possible in a neat, substantial and workmanlike manner. The walls have already been run about nine feet. On this spot are shingles, brick and lime, enough it is thought to complete the work. All other materials with such of those as may be found not sufficiently good are to be provided by the undertaker; who will have to give bond, with undoubted security, for the faithful performance of this contract.[18]

The Scottish traveler John Melish gave a good description of the state house when he visited Louisville in 1806. It shows that the real building turned out to be very much as it was proposed. He said:

It is a good building of brick, about 50 feet square and consist of two stories, having three apartments each and a large lobby. The House of Representatives meet in an apartment on the lower floor and the other two are occupied as a secretary's office and the land office. The upper story consists of the Senate chamber, executive office and the treasury.[19]

Even as the state house was completed, there were some other problems for the commissioners of Louisville. It appears that the Georgia government had not been giving them money to pay for all the materials and work that was being done. The result was that the commissioners were sued and judgments obtained against them for the sum of more than £200 "including interest and costs for articles furnished and work done in the said State-house."[20]

A committee appointed by the Houses of Representatives reviewed the records and work of Hugh Lawson and John Shelman, the late commissioners of Louisville. They observed that the prices that the commissioners allowed for some of the work done and articles furnished were very high, but they had reason to believe that these articles at that time and under those circumstances could not have been obtained on better terms. The committee found a contract entered into by Robert Forsyth and James Jones, late commissioners of Louisville, agreeing to pay Reuben Coleman the sum of £1,890 for finishing the state house. The committee also learned that the state house would be finished within two months and that there would be due to the administrators of Reuben Coleman's estate, a sum of more than £592.[21]

Even as the state house was finished, many changes and improvements had to be made with the building. Only a year after the state house was completed, one Joseph Rees was paid $100 for putting up new "frontis pieces etc." in the state house.[22]

A year later, Governor James Jackson noticed that many animals were coming around the state house. Because of this, on 17 January 1798, he recommended that the state house be enclosed and stated that:

> I conceive this enclosure to be necessary for the preservation of the house itself which has cost so large a sum to erect. Nothing stamps so strong an impression of public character as the state of public buildings. An enclosure will prevent horses, cattle, etc, from approaching it whilst the front rail end will afford an agreeable walk for the members during the sitting of the legislator [*sic*] and the citizens of Louisville during the recess.[23]

During the next month, Governor Jackson raised concerns about what was happening with this enclosure. He wrote the commissioners of Louisville and asked for information about the progress and price of this project so that it could "be ascertained whether or not this work should be continued."[24] This letter brought about an order from the executive department on 17 February 1798 to investigate the contract for this project and to stop the work on it until an investigation could be completed.[25]

A year after the discussion on the enclosure of the state house began, Governor Jackson wrote to the executive department that although the

> contract was not perfect, and a brick wall would have been preferable as being more durable, yet as the work as it is, adds respectability to the state building an equitable price should be allowed the workman—the sum contracted for appeared to me to be extravagant but you are better judges than myself, and may not deem it unreasonable.[26]

Later in that same year, the executive department recommended that sets of lightning rods or conductors be erected against the two chimneys of the state house.[27]

Even with these improvements, the state house still could not be considered a very good or safe building. This is made quite clear in a report that John Berrien, the state treasurer, made to the Executive Department of the State of Georgia. His report discussed the safety and security of his office, and he found that the doors of the rooms are paneled and consequently very insecure for an office which is the deposit of so large a sum as it is at present under charge of the treasurer. The windows are also very insufficient, the shutters are venetian and of course not calculated for security against plunderers. The walls are still more vulnerable than either the doors or the windows being nothing more than common laths and plaster that might at any time be cut through with a common knife in three minutes which renders the office extremely insecure even in the daytime when the officers retire to breakfast or dinner. The facility with which a person intend upon mischief might even cut his way through the floor from the Surveyors General's office into the treasury if an additional proof of the want of security to the latter office.[28]

Realizing that little could be done to improve the security of the building from a structural standpoint, the executive department decided that four people should be hired to guard the state house. One person was to be hired at a dollar a night to command and direct the detail. The other three were to act as "watchmen" and were paid a half dollar each night. With this solution, Georgians could now feel more at ease about the security of the state documents and monies.[29]

As can be seen, the commissioners of Louisville were given a great deal of authority, but they also faced some real problems. One problem was disorderliness in the town of Louisville. A law was passed on 31 January 1798 giving the commissioners special powers to better regulate Louisville. The law appointed Doctor John Powell, John Berrien, Chesley Bostwick, John Shelman, and Michael Shelman as commissioners of Louisville. They were given full power and authority to "make such by-laws and regulations, and inflict or impose such pains, penalties and forfeitures as shall be conducive to the good order and government of the said town of Louisville."[30]

The filling of commissioner positions and the length of their terms also presented problems. In the executive department minutes of 29 February 1798, it is noted that Michael Shelman and Nicolas Long had executive appointments and that these appointments expired at the end of the next session of the General Assembly. However, they were never confirmed by the legislature. After this time the validity of any decisions made by them was questioned.[31]

Because of legal questions about the authority of some of the commissioners to sell lots, the legislature felt it necessary to validate the titles on all lots sold by the Commissioner of Louisville. On 8 February 1799, the following bill was passed: "to confirm and make valid all titles to certain lots sold by the commissioners of the town of Louisville."[32]

In 1801, the commissioners were given additional power to lay off all the remaining land belonging to Louisville, except what was necessary for commons, into "lots of such size as they may deem expedient; and may from time to time, lease the same for such term as they may think fit."[33]

The legislature also gave the commissioners of Louisville the responsibility of disposing of the alleys and part of several streets in Louisville. On 10 December 1803 an act was passed by the Georgia assembly that noted that the alleys in Louisville, had not served the "beneficial purpose for which they were intended, and the inhabitants thereof, conceive them to be a disadvantage, and dangerous to their health." To remedy this situation, the commissioners of Louisville were "to sell and dispose of the said alleys." The people who owned lots adjoining the alleys were to be given the right to purchase half or all of the alley next to them, and if they did not buy this land, it was to be disposed of at public sale to the highest bidder.

This law also empowered the commissioners "to dispose to the highest bidder," certain parts of Mulberry, Walnut, and Peach streets. The money arising from these sales of alleys and parts of streets was to be given to the "commissioners of the Academy in the said town, to be applied towards the repairs and for the benefit of the said Academy."[34] Apparently the commissioners had problems finishing their work on this matter, so another law was passed on 13 December 1804 extending their time to sell these alleys until 10 December 1805.[35]

The Establishment of a New County

After the legislature began meeting in Louisville, almost as an after-thought, the decision was made that a new county should be laid out around the site of Georgia's new capital. A petition had actually been given to the House of Representatives by some inhabitants of the counties of Warren, Burke, Montgomery, and Washington "praying the establishment of a new county out of the several counties aforesaid," and this petition was referred to a special committee.[36] Most of modern Jefferson County was originally part of early Burke County, which had been the colonial parish of St. George.

By an act on 20 February 1796, the Georgia legislature established a new county, which was named for Thomas Jefferson, the author of the Declaration of Independence and third president of the United States. This act read as follows:

> That a new county shall be laid out of part of the counties of Burke and Warren, in manner and form following, to wit, beginning at Hargrave's bridge on the River Ogeechee, from thence running in a direct line to Pegg's old field, thence in a direct line to Ballard's mill, thence in a direct line to the Chickasaw bridge or ford on Brier Creek, thence up the stream of the said creek to Harris' bridge; thence on a direct line to the mouth of Big Creek, where it makes a confluence with the river Ogeechee aforesaid, thence down Ogeechee to the western line of the Big Survey, thence across Ogeechee River a direct line to run to the mouth of the first branch above Vivion's bridge on Williamson's swamp, thence across said swamp in a direct line to where the Sunbury line strikes the Montgomery line, thence down the said road to the Hurricane, thence along said Hurricane eastwardly to Williamson's swamp, thence down the said swamp to Reuben Hargrave's bridge the place of beginning; which county shall be called and known by the name of Jefferson.[37]

After the creation of Jefferson County, its government began to get organized, and soon it was operational. By midsummer of 1796, some parts of the county government were organized. John Shelman, Douglas Hancock, Solomon Wood, Michael Shelman, and John Clements were appointed as justices of the Inferior Court. They met for the first time on 11 July 1796, concerning themselves principally with roads and bridges.[38]

The justices of the Inferior Court were authorized by the law to levy a tax on the people of the county for the building of a courthouse and a jail. The law appointed Michael Shelman; John M. Sterret; Chesley Bostwick, junior; John Barron; and John Parsons as commissioners for erecting a courthouse and jail, with full power to contract for the construction of these buildings. The law also specified that "the place of holding courts and elections for the county of Jefferson, shall be in the town of Louisville in the house of Joseph Chairs until a court-house shall be erected."[39]

Apparently not much progress was made in building a courthouse or jail for Jefferson County, because in an act passed on 4 December 1801 the situation remained about the same. The legislature made a decision, however, to remove the courts and elections from the house of Joseph

Chairs, and the justices of the inferior court were "authorized and empowered to fix on some fit and convenient house in the town of Louisville, in which Courts and Elections for said county of Jefferson shall be held, until a Court-House shall be erected." At this time, John Clements, John Shelman, William Flemming, and Alexander Caswell were appointed "Commissioners of the Court-House and Gaol, for the County of Jefferson."[40]

On 8 March 1802, acting in pursuance of an act of the legislature of 1801, the justices of the inferior court, with the consent of the governor, decided on the state house "as a fit and convenient place for holding court and elections." A few months later, however, courts and elections were ordered held at the house of Jonathan Hilton in Louisville. It is likely, nevertheless, that the state house was used when the general assembly was not in session.[41]

As early as 1797, the executive department awarded $428.17 "in favor of the Commissioners of the Court House and Jail for the County of Jefferson."[42] In 1799 the House of Representatives put forth a bill "for appropriating part of the commons of vacant lots of the Town of Louisville for the purpose of erecting a court house."[43] On 8 December 1806 the state passed a law to "empower the Inferior Court of Jefferson County to levy an extra tax, for the purpose of building a new jail in the county."[44] It was not until much later, however, that a courthouse and jail were actually built in Jefferson County.

Taxes in Louisville and Jefferson County

To provide the money for the government of Louisville and Jefferson County to operate, the county levied taxes on land, slaves, carriages, liquor stills, pool tables, and many other things. These taxes were not only an inconvenience to the people of the area but in many cases completely destroyed them financially.

In contrast to today, liquor stills were legal. You could make all the whisky you wanted, but you were supposed to register your still with the county and pay taxes on it. The following article appeared in the Louisville newspaper of 1800:

> Every person having a still or stills within the county of Jefferson, are requested to make entry of the same before the first day of July next, at the office of inspection, in Louisville, agreeable to an act of Congress. The penalty to be inflicted on those who neglect to make

entry as aforesaid, is two hundred and fifty dollars. If any have stills not intended for use they must be entered accordingly.[45]

In early Louisville taxes were also levied on carriages, wagons, and other modes of transportation. The *State Gazette and Louisville Journal* of 1799 listed some sixteen different types of taxable vehicles on which one had to pay as much as $15 for a coach or as little as $2 for a two-wheel carriage.[46]

The most highly taxed item was a billiard table. Apparently, only one billiard table existed in Louisville during its early days. For whatever reason, a very high tax was put on this table, making it virtually impossible for a person to keep this table for very long. There is a notice of a "Collector's sale" of one billiard table of Joseph Fletcher for $100 in 1800[47] and one of Eli Browning for $100 in taxes in 1801.[48] It is interesting that the tax on 10,000 acres of land was $22.68 but the tax on one billiard table was $100. Apparently the community really wanted to get rid of this billiard table, yet it kept appearing at the collector's sales for several years.

The tax that people disliked the most and the one that hurt them the most was the tax on land. Although these taxes were very low, only a few cents or less an acre, money was very scarce, and many people just did not have the few dollars in cash that were necessary to pay their taxes. One collector's sale of 1804 offered 112 acres of pine land on Rocky Comfort Creek for $.54 tax; 237 1/2 acres of second-quality land in Jefferson County on the Ogeechee River for $5.23 tax; 200 acres of second-quality and 217 acres of third-quality land on Rocky Comfort Creek for $6.87 1/2 tax; and 30 acres of pine land on Rocky Comfort Creek for $.43 tax.[49] Even really large tracts of land were sold to pay off small amounts of taxes. A notice also appeared for the sale of "10,000 acres in Franklin and Jackson Counties on Oconee River as property of Peter J. Carnes deceased for taxes of $22.68."[50]

Most of the tax digests of Jefferson County have been preserved since 1796, and the ones from this early period provide some valuable information about what was happening in Louisville and Jefferson County at that time. During 1796, 636 households in Jefferson County owned land and 138 did not. These households paid $1,132.87 in property taxes, the largest tax being the $108.80 paid by John Shelman for the estate of Abijah Dows, who owned 80,000 acres in Franklin County. Most people paid taxes of a dollar or less. In the county 164 households (26%) owned slaves. There were 766 slaves counted for tax purposes, and the largest slave owner in Jefferson County was Tom Lewis, who had 60 slaves. Most people in this county did not own slaves, and those who did generally had a very small number. It should also be mentioned that some 90 Jefferson County households also owned land in other Georgia counties.[51]

The tax digests also contain a list of everyone that owned lots in Louisville and how many they owned. Forty-four people owned 81½ lots. Thirty-nine of those lot owners lived in Louisville.[52]

Jefferson County, according to the information contained in the 1801 tax digest, had 793 households. Among these, 112 (14%) owned additional land outside Jefferson County, and 258 households (33%) owned slaves. They had a total of 1,403 slaves.[53]

In 1801 the largest tax payers in the county were Eli Browning, who paid $100.34 for 7¼ acres of land and one billiard table; Robert Flournoy, who paid $38.45 for 30,000 acres of land and 37 slaves; and John Lewis, who paid $27.75 for 850 acres and 79 slaves.[54] As can be seen, one suffered a considerable tax penalty for owning a billiard table.

When one looks at the 1804 tax digest, one finds that some changes were taking place in Louisville and Jefferson County. All the taxpayers in the county paid a total of $1,593.28 in taxes. Interestingly, the total tax received in 1799 was $1,946.43, or $353.15 more than in 1804. The reason for this decline probably relates to the fact that by this time the legislature had decided to move the capital from Louisville to Milledgeville. This proposed relocation must have disturbed the merchants and landowners alike and caused them considerable worry about the future value of their investments.[55]

The 1804 tax digest also shows that Jefferson County had 799 households (compared with 748 in 1799), of whom 95 (12%) owned land outside the county (compared with 110 in 1799). Of those households, 296 (37%) households (compared with 223 in 1799) owned a total of 1708 slaves (compared with 1,213 in 1799) Thus there was an increase in the number of landowners and slaves, but decreases in the amount of tax and the number of people owning land outside the county.[56]

The largest taxpayer in the county was Robert Flournoy, who paid $50.65 for 70 slaves and 25,000 acres of land. He was followed closely by Samuel Vichers, who paid $50.31 for one billiard table and no land. The next largest taxpayer was John Lewis, who paid $23.43 for 69 slaves and 950 acres of land.[57]

As for the city of Louisville, many changes were taking place, because the Georgia legislature had decided to move the seat of the government to Milledgeville. Land owners and store owners alike were trying to decide on how this move would impact on them. If one compares who owned lots in Louisville in 1801 and in 1804, he/she finds many new names in 1804 and the disappearance of many of the 1801 lot owners. The store owners also changed a great deal. Louisville had more people, new stores, and an uncertain future.[58]

Militia Groups of Louisville and Jefferson County

The people of Louisville and Jefferson County had experienced many problems with the Indians in earlier days, and because of this they did not feel comfortable without a well organized military unit in their midst. In addition to this, the founding and development of Louisville and Jefferson County took place only a few years after the American Revolution. Because fighting had taken place in every part of Georgia during this period, most men were a part of some military group. When the war was over and the Indians were pushed further to the west, the local military units did not stop functioning, but rather they continued to play a very important role in the towns and counties throughout Georgia.

Many different militia groups were in Louisville and Jefferson County. Almost every man in the county was a member of one of these military units, which were very active in the early life of the area. These military units frequently held parades and put on mock battles for the people of the area, particularly on American Independence Day. In the activities of 4 July 1799, during the afternoon, a sham fight took place between Major Scott's battalion, Captain Connolly's horse, and the artillery. During the exercise, Captain Connolly and one of his men were shot because of "their horses not being properly trained to martial exercise." After the sham fight, the militia went to the state house to drink "porter and spirits" prepared for them by the governor and Major Scott. The artillery went to the Coffee House and ate an excellent dinner, prepared for the occasion. One of the participants commented about "the happy and social manner, which ever characterizes true republicans."[59]

The Louisville and Jefferson artillery companies were apparently more show than substance, because they seemingly had only one artillery piece and only fired it on important occasions. They pulled their big gun around much more in parades than they fired it. When they were allowed to fire their cannon, usually enough powder for only sixteen rounds was given to them.[60] One important day in May 1798, they were asked to fire their gun to "announce the signing" of the new Georgia Constitution.[61]

The militia groups also had formal activities on General George Washington's birthday. The Louisville newspaper of 1800 reported that the "Louisville Artillery Company ushered in the morn, by a discharge of 16 guns. Half hour guns were fired through the day." In addition to this, "Major Scott's Battalion and Captain Connolly's Company of Horse marched from Mr. Posner's to the Jefferson Academy where an oration was delivered by Peter J. Carnes.[62]

At the funeral ceremonies of important people, the militia groups likewise played an important role. At the death of Representative James Jones, the Louisville artillery paraded in front of Jefferson Academy where "the Governor of the State and County Officers, civil and military, together with such citizens as choose to attend" were assembled. They formed a procession there during which the artillery group fired "minute guns" "to the number of his years of age." After "a suitable eulogium on the melancholy occasion" was delivered at the state house by one of the students of the academy, the newspaper says that they fired sixteen rounds from the artillery to complete the ceremony.[63]

The local calvary unit was called the Jefferson Troop of Light Horse or the Jefferson Troop of Light Dragoons, and they frequently displayed their equestrian skills. At every possible occasion, they paraded in the streets of Louisville and seemed to enjoy the attention of the local crowds.[64] After the death of the Revolutionary War hero Patrick Carr near Louisville, members of the local calvary unit and other interested citizens gathered at Carr's grave for speeches. Afterwards the local calvary "displayed a variety of equestrian evolutions appropriate to the occasion and ended the martial ceremony with a regular discharge by platoons."[65]

One should not think that the activities of the local militias were all ceremonial, because they were also used to maintain peace and enforce the law in Louisville and Jefferson County. Executive department minutes of 1798, recorded that

> General Scott will order out a party of calvary to support the sheriff of Jefferson County, in the legal execution of his duty--the said sheriff having represented that it is out of his power to serve several criminal processes now in his possession without aid from the military.[66]

In 1799, the militia groups were used "to patrol the street of Louisville every night until after the meeting of the legislature and to apprehend all disorderly and suspicious persons that may be found lurking about the town."[67] This action was taken after someone attempted to burn down the town.[68] On several occasions the militias were also used to guard prisoners at the jail of Jefferson County.[69] When Garland Hardwick, the tax collector of Jefferson County, tried to collect a levy on one Nathan Powell for several slaves, Powell threatened him "with a leaded whip." Major Henry J. Caldwell then assigned a noncommissioned officer and six privates "to protect and support" Mr. Hardwick in his work.[70]

Important Governmental Events in Louisville the Capital

Because it was the capital, many important governmental events took place in Louisville between 1796 and 1807. The most important thing, of course, was the fact that the legislature met there and the governors resided there.

The first legislature to meet in Louisville was on the second Tuesday in January, the twelfth day of 1796.[71] It should be noted that the state house was listed as being in Augusta until 29 December 1795; it began to be in Louisville on 9 January 1796.[72] The state house stayed in Louisville until the end of 1806. A Savannah newspaper noted that the legislature of Georgia was in session in Louisville in November of 1806.[73] The Executive Department of Georgia was still meeting in Louisville as late as the last of March of 1807.[74]

The governors who held office during the time that Louisville was the capital were Jared Irwin (1796–1798 and 1806–1809), James Jackson (1798–1801), David Emanuel (1801), Josiah Tattnall (1801–1802), and John Milledge (1802–1806).[75]

The Constitutional Conventions of 1795 and 1798

As a new state, it was necessary for Georgia to evaluate its constitution and laws regularly and make needed changes. Consecutive constitutional conventions were held in 1777, 1778, and 1789. The constitution of 1789 was the most carefully considered, but it was of short duration. It contained a provision that at the general election in 1794 the freemen of the state should select delegates to a convention who should take into consideration needed alterations in the constitution.[76]

Actually, a constitutional convention met in Louisville before the first legislature convened there. This convention met in Louisville in May

1795 and spent most of its time debating the apportionment for senators
and representatives in the different counties. Additionally, it decided that
the General Assembly was to meet annually on the second Tuesday of
January, instead of the first Monday in November; that the seat of
government was to be removed from Augusta to Louisville; and that
provisions were to be made for further changes of the constitution in
1798.[77]

The fifty-six delegates elected to the 1798 convention, representing
twenty-one counties, met in Louisville, on Tuesday, 8th May. The convention resolved to take into consideration the constitution and amend-
ments, section by section. It met as a group until the 30th of May. All
propositions were first discussed in the committee of the whole, and then
reported to the convention, which took final action upon them. The
constitution that resulted from this convention remained in force for
sixty-three years.[78]

The Great Seal of Georgia

The legislature passed an act on 8 February 1799 to alter the Great Seal
of the State of Georgia. It called on artists to submit drawings for the
proposed new "Great Seal of the State." A premium of thirteen dollars
was to be given for the best drawing for the new seal.[79] The drawings
were due in the executive office at Louisville on or before 20 April 179.

At the same time, proposals were to be submitted for making and
engraving the device; 3 July 1799 was fixed as the deadline to complete
the contract. Daniel Sturgis, state surveyor general, made the device
approved by the governor for the seal.[80]

The seal that was adopted was a disc, two and one-quarter inches in
diameter. On one side it had a view of a seashore, with a ship bearing the
flag of the United States riding at anchor near a wharf and receiving on
board hogsheads of tobacco and bales of cotton, emblematic of the
exports of the state. At a little distance was a boat landing from the
interior of the state with hogsheads, boxes, and other items, representing
internal traffic. In the background was a man plowing and a flock of
sheep under the shade of a tree. The motto on this side was "Agriculture
and Commerce 1799."On the reverse side were three pillars supporting
an arch, with the word "Constitution" engraved on it. It was supported
by the three departments of government (legislative, judicial, and
executive). The words, "Wisdom, Justice, and Moderation," were

engraved on the base of each of these pillars, one word on each pillar. On the right of the last pillar was a man standing with a drawn sword representing the aid of the military in defense of the constitution. The inscription on this side of the seal was "State of Georgia 1799."[81]

When it was made, the "Great Seal" was deposited in the office of the secretary of state, to be attached to all official papers of Georgia. The old seal was formally broken in the presence of the governor. A newspaper of 1799 described this important event:

> At one o'clock, the law respecting the Great Seal of the State was read by Horation Marbury, esq., The Old Seal was broke by order of the Governor, and the new one delivered by him to the Secretary of State; after which the artillery again fired a federal salute.[82]

The Yazoo Fraud

One of the most famous events ever to have occurred in Louisville was the overturning of the Yazoo Act and the burning of the "Yazoo Fraud Papers." Most people, however, are not familiar with what the Yazoo Act and Fraud really were and the significance they had for Georgia.

To understand these things, one must look back to how the boundary lines of early Georgia changed. In 1752, Georgia became an English royal colony in control of a limited amount of land between the Savannah and the Altamaha Rivers, but the western boundary of Georgia was thought to be in the middle of the Mississippi River. When Great Britain signed the peace treaty with the United States in 1783, it recognized all of this land as belonging to Georgia. In that same year, the Georgia legislature opened a land office, and it defined the state boundaries as extending from the Savannah River to the Mississippi River. Thus in 1783, Georgia was in control not only of the area in what is now the state of Georgia, but it also possessed most of Alabama and Mississippi.

The land between the Chattahoochee and Mississippi Rivers became involved in the Yazoo Fraud. As businessmen and "confidence" men realized the existence of this "Yazoo country" (which was named after the Yazoo River in that area) and its potential for development and profit, a fever of land speculation began to run wild in the United States and many schemes were devised to purchase Georgia's land.

Speculation in Georgia's western lands began almost as soon as independence came, and a new land scheme appeared almost every year.[83] In 1788 Georgia actually offered to sell a strip 140 miles wide and stretching from the Chattahoochee River to the Mississippi River to the U.S. Congress on condition that the state be paid $171,428.45, which had been the cost of quieting the Indians. The Georgia legislature also specified that the U.S. Congress should confirm its claims to all the other land within her boundary. This offer and a counter offer by the U.S. Congress were both rejected.[84]

In 1789, Georgia decided to sell its western land to three groups of speculators. These groups bargained for three separate pieces of territory, which they thought at the time to consist of about 15,000,000 acres, but which was later changed to 20,000,000 acres. For this land the speculators agreed to pay a total of $207,000 within two years.

By impressing the Georgia legislators with the importance of selling the vacant land and applying the proceeds to pay off the state debt, the schemers were able to get a bill through the state legislature. The terms of the bill required a small cash payment, and other payments extending over a period of two years. If, however, the last payment was not made at the end of two years, the land was again to become the property of the state of Georgia.[85]

The sale was much disliked throughout Georgia and became an issue in the state elections the next year. The majority of the members elected to the legislature were opposed to the sale, particularly since payments for the land were offered in worthless paper money. Georgia refused to accept the payments and at the end of two years again declared its right to the Yazoo land that had been sold.[86]

It might seem that Georgia, having escaped selling a vast amount of its land for about a penny an acre, would have been slow to part with a greater area at an even smaller price. Georgia officials, however, were induced, mainly through bribery, to make a second Yazoo sale in 1795. This time four companies were organized, and each was allotted a roughly defined tract at a definite price. Since these boundaries had not been surveyed, no one knew how many acres were being sold, but the estimates ran from 35,000,000 to 50,000,000 acres. The total price offered by the four companies was $500,000, or about one to one-and-a-half cents an acre.

These land speculators developed a deep-seated plot to corrupt the legislature of Georgia. The trusted representatives of the people of Georgia and of other states swarmed into Augusta to hurry this law through the legislature by bribing, threatening, and persuading. James Gunn, a United States senator from Georgia, was one of the chief lobbyists. Bribes of land as much as 75,000 acres to one person, of slaves, of barrels of rice, and of money were freely handed out to those legislators whose consciences inclined them against the bill. Some who were too honest to vote for the bill were induced to go home.

Governor George Matthews initially refused to sign the bill for the land sale, but the Yazooists somewhat modified their offer, executed some parliamentary maneuvers, and induced the governor to sign the bill. It should be noted that all the members of the Georgia legislature who voted for this sale, except one, had shares in the companies who bought the land.[87]

As news of the Yazoo land sale swept across Georgia in 1795, it caused one of the wildest scenes ever witnessed in the state. Some people brought ropes to hang the members of the legislature who favored the sale, and it was only the influence of the minority who opposed the sale that actually prevented bloodshed. Because of these unexpected actions, the Georgia legislature adjourned in confusion, and members who had voted for the sale fled to other states or concealed themselves in their own counties. One state senator was actually followed into South Carolina and killed.[88]

The Yazoo sale became the only political issue for the state elections of 1796. Georgia leaders who favored the sale were ostracized, while any man who opposed the sale became an immediate leader. Senator James Jackson, who opposed the sale, felt so strongly about the situation that he resigned his seat in the United States Senate and was elected as a state representative from Chatham County. He then took the lead in the fight against the Yazoo Act. In fact, every man that was elected in 1796 in Georgia pledged to support a bill for rescinding the Yazoo sale.[89]

In the election of 1796, the corrupt legislature was turned out and a new group assembled in Louisville, the new capital, determined to wipe out every vestige of the shame that had been heaped upon the state. There the first matter of business for the legislature was the Yazoo land sale. The House of Representatives appointed a committee to examine and report respecting the validity and constitutionality of the Act. This committee met with many obstacles and was threatened with violence, but they were not men to be intimidated by threats or turned aside from their duty by the rage of those who opposed their actions. This committee put forth the propositions that the land sale was made illegally, was dishonorable to the state, and was contradictory to the Georgia constitution. Therefore they declared the Yazoo Act and land sale null and void, and they made provisions to repay the amounts paid by the purchasers. The bill was passed by a vote of forty-four to three in the House, and fourteen to four in the Senate, and was approved by the governor on 13 February 1796.[90]

Having repealed this notorious land sale, the Georgia legislature decided to have a public burning of the act that had made the sale possible. The date was set for 13 February 1796, and on this day people from all parts of the state came to Louisville. Numerous stories were told about the burning of the Yazoo papers, but probably the most credible one was about a fire that was built in front of the state house. According to this story, members of the House and Senate examined the act, passed it to the Speaker of the House, who read it and passed it to the clerk, who handed it to the door-keeper, who committed it to the flames. Tradition says that the fire was drawn from heaven by means of a sun glass in order to make the scene more impressive.[91]

Considering all the problems Georgia had experienced with the Yazoo land sales, the state decided to make a final settlement of its western territory with the United States government. In 1802, James Jackson, Abraham Baldwin, and John Milledge were appointed as Georgia commissioners. They met with the United States commissioner and agreed to give up all Georgia's territory west of the Chattahoochee River. In return Georgia was to receive $1,250,000 and that part of the South Carolina cession to the United States that lay east of Georgia's western boundary.

A result of the Yazoo scandal in Georgia was the birth of strong and bitter political factions. The followers of Jackson became the bearers of the Jeffersonian and States Rights standards in Georgia politics for the next two decades, and the Yazooists tended to become Federalists.[92] Jackson was in reality the founder of the first genuine political party in Georgia, the party led by William H. Crawford and George M. Troup after Jackson's death. It should also be noted that the Yazoo dispute became a national issue after 1802, and for a dozen years it disrupted and embittered American politics.[93]

The Yazoo Fraud was not quietly forgotten in Louisville, as can be clearly seen by an article in the local newspaper of 1801:

> Died here a few days ago after a short illness General Yazoo, a man universally regretted by a late numerous class of society. . . . His disorder it is rumored was of the bilious kind, but others assert it arose from the flavia of certain papers burnt some time past in the vicinity of

the house where he departed. . . . No assistance which the most profound medical aid could give was wanting to restore once more to the arms of his beloved coadjutors, the standing army and land speculating gentry their sincere friend.[94]

This material clearly indicates that governmental life in Louisville was very active during this period. These were "glorious days" for Louisville as it received all the attention as the seat of the government for the state of Georgia. The daily life of the town at this time was equally as exciting and active, and this made these days even more glorious for Louisville.

Notes

[1]Warren Grice and E. Merton Coulter, eds., *Georgia Through Two Centuries* (New York: Lewis Historical Publishing Co., 1965) 1:382.

[2]Lucien E. Roberts, "Sectional Problems in Georgia during the Formative Period, 1776–1798," *Georgia Historical Quarterly* 18/3 (1934): 209.

[3]"Three Isaac Briggs Letters," *Georgia Historical Quarterly* 12/1 (1928): 178-79.

[4]Robert and George Watkins, *Digest of the Laws of the State of Georgia from the Beginning to 1800* (Savannah: 1802) 320-21.

[5]*CRG*, XIX, Pt. II, 466-68.　　　　[6]Ibid., 133.

[7]*Augusta Chronicle and Gazette of the State* (Augusta), 9 May 1789.

[8]Watkins, *Digest*, 321.

[9]Lucius Q. C. Lamar, *A Compilation of the Laws of the State of Georgia, 1810 through 1819* (Augusta 1821) 971.

[10]Virginia Polhill Price, "Louisville: Georgia's First Capital," *The Georgia Review* 6 (Spring 1952): 31.

[11]Mrs. Z. V. Thomas, *History of Jefferson County* (Spartanburg SC: The Reprint Company, 1978) 36-37. See also Marion Little Durden, *A History of Saint George Parish Colony of Georgia, Jefferson County State of Georgia* (Swainsboro GA: Magnolia Press, 1983).

[12]Knight, *Georgia's Landmarks*, 147.

[13]Thomas, *History*, 116.

[14]*Gazette of the State of Georgia*, 19 April 1787. One might note the unusual spelling "Lewisville" for Louisville. This is the only time that the writer found it spelled this way.

[15]*Augusta Chronicle and Gazette of the State*, 24 August 1793.　[16]Ibid.

[17]Watkins, *Digest*, 20 Dec 1793, 536.

[18]*Augusta Chronicle and Gazette of the State*, 24 August 1793.

[19]John Melish, *Travels Through the United States of America in the Years 1806, 1807, and 1808, 1810 and 1811* (Philadelphia, 1815) 1:39-46.

[20]*House of Representatives Journal*, 12 Jan 1796–11 January 1797, 111.

[21]Ibid., 112-13.

[22]*Executive Department Minutes*, 5 August 1797, 243.

[23]Ibid., 13 October 1797–28 June 1798, 73.   [24]Ibid., 163.

[25]Ibid., 162. See also MSS no. 279 in the Georgia Historical Society Collection.   [26]Ibid., 341.   [27]Ibid., 22 June 1798, 394.

[28]Ibid., 140.   [29]Ibid., 141.

[30]Watkins, *Digest*, 673.

[31]*Executive Department Minutes*, 13 October 1797–28 June 1798, 172-73.

[32]*House of Representative Journal*, 8 February 1799, 56; Augustin Smith Clayton, *A Compilation of the Laws of the State of Georgia, Passed by the Legislature since the Political Year 1800, to the Year 1810* (Augusta: Adams and Duyckinck, 1813) 672.

[33]*House of Representatives Journal*, 4 December 1801, 68.

[34]Clayton, *Compilation*, 126.   [35]Ibid., 207.

[36]*House of Representatives Journal*, 25 January 1796, 34, and 17 January 1797, 193, and 198.

[37]Horatio Marbury and William H. Crawford, *Digest of the Laws of the State of Georgia* (Savannah: Seymour, Woolhopter, and Stebbins, 1802) 169-70.

[38]*Inferior Court Minutes*, 1: 1796-1800, 2-6.

[39]Marbury and Crawford, *Digest*, 179. [40]Clayton, *Compilation*, 19.

[41]*Inferior Court Minutes*, 2: 1800-1803, 100-101 and 112.

[42]Executive Department Minutes, 19 April 1797, 176.

[43]*House of Representatives Journal*, 12 February 1799, 64.

[44]Clayton, *Compilation*, 317-18.

[45]*Louisville Gazette and Republican Trumpet*, 10 June 1800. Hereafter this newspaper will be abbreviated LGRT.

[46]*State Gazette and Louisville Journal*, 10 September 1799; Also see LGRT, 23 Sept 1800.

[47]*LGRT*, 19 November 1800.

[48]Ibid., 2 May 1801 and 23 March 1802.   [49]Ibid., 8 August 1804.

[50]Ibid., 10 February 1802.

[51]*Jefferson County Tax Digest*, 1796.   [52]Ibid., 1796.

[53]Ibid., 1801.   [54]Ibid.   [55]Ibid., 1804.

[56]Ibid., 1804 and 1799.   [57]Ibid., 1804.   [58]Ibid.

[59]*Louisville Gazette*, 9 July 1799; See also LGRT, 11 July 1804. Hereafter *Louisville Gazette* will abbreviated LG.

[60]*Executive Department Minutes*, 8 November 1799–14 November 1800, 310.

[61]Ibid., 28 May 1798, 324.

[62]*LG*, 25 February 1800.

[63]*LGRT,* 7 February 1801.

[64]Ibid., 11 April 1801; 11 May 1803.

[65]Ibid., 29 December 1802; 18 December 1802.

[66]*Executive Department Minutes,* 17 September 1798, 175.

[67]Ibid., 6 January 1797, 50.

[68]Ibid., 30 December 1796, 49.

[69]Ibid., 3 October 1798, 217, and 29 October 1800, 499.

[70]Ibid., 2 May 1800, 286 and 300.

[71]*Journal of the House of Representatives,* 12 January 1796–11 February 1797, 1.

[72]*Executive Department Minutes,* 3 November 1793–23 September 1796, 334.

[73]*Columbian Museum and Savannah Advertiser* 12 November 1806.

[74]*LGRT,* 20 March 1807.

[75]George White, *Statistics of the State of Georgia* (Savannah: W. Thorne Williams, 1849) 59.

[76]Grice, *Georgia Through Two Centuries* 1:291.

[77]Amanda Johnson, "A State in the Making," *Georgia Historical Quarterly* 15/1 (March 1931): 1-27.

[78]William Bacon Stevens, *A History of Georgia* (Philadelphia: E. H. Butler and Co., 1859) 2:498-500.

[79]Henry R. Goetchies, "The Great Seals of Georgia: Their Origin and History," *Georgia Historical Quarterly* 1/3 (1917): 261; *LG,* 26 February 1799.

[80]Ibid., 262.   [81]Ibid., 262.

[82]*LG,* 9 July 1799.

[83]E. Merton Coulter, *Georgia: A Short History* (Chapel Hill: University of North Carolina Press, 1960) 199-200.

[84]William Estill Heath, "The Yazoo Land Fraud," *Georgia Historical Quarterly* 16/4 (December 1932): 278.

[85]Ibid., 279.   [86]Ibid.   [87]Ibid., 281.

[88]White, *Statistics,* 50.

[89]Coulter, *Georgia,* 202; Alexander A. Lawrence, "James Jackson: Passionate Patriot," *Georgia Historical Quarterly* 34/2 (June 1950): 79.

[90]Ibid., 202; Grice, *Georgia Through Two Centuries,* 1:147.

[91]Heath, "The Yazoo Land Fraud," 282.

[92]Roberts, "Sectional Problems in Georgia," 224.

[93]Coulter, Georgia, 205 and 238.

[94]*LGRT,* 8 September 1801.

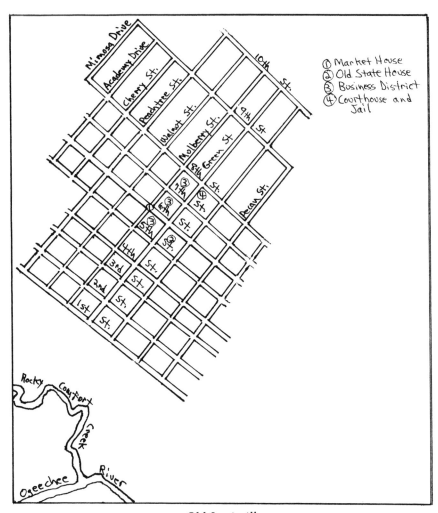

Old Louisville

3
Daily Life in Louisville the Capital

In addition to being a vibrant place from a governmental standpoint, Louisville as Georgia's capital was also a center of economic, cultural, educational, social, and religious life in the state. It was likewise a rather rowdy place in which to live on many occasions.

Safety in Louisville

Louisville, as a new town and Georgia's new capital, attracted the very best of Georgia's population, but it also attracted some of the worst elements who came looking for excitement or for opportunities to strike it rich. The fighting, killing, and looting during the Revolutionary War had left the people that survived very tough, and many of these people lived rather wild and riotous lives. Life in the early days of Louisville and Jefferson County saw fights, duels, street racing, and freely flowing whiskey.

Things got particularly rough around the time of the legislative sessions. The most violent times came in connection with the legislature of 1797. Just before the session began, someone apparently tried to burn down the whole town of Louisville, including the state house. As a result of this action, the Executive Department of Georgia gave the following order on 30 December 1796: "In consequence of the late attempt to fire this town, it is ordered that the treasurer be authorized to augment the guard at the state house to six men, and to cause a centinel [*sic*] to be constantly on duty from sunset until sunrise until farther [*sic*] orders." They were not satisfied that this was adequate to protect the town or the legislators, so on 6 January 1797, the executive department directed Majors Caldwell and Scott

> to order parties of militia to patrol the streets of Louisville every night until after the meeting of the legislature and to apprehend all disorderly and suspicious persons that may be found lurking about the town.[1]

A few days later, the *Columbian Museum and Savannah Advertiser* gave a story about a fire that was set at the house of John Berrien but was discovered before it did any damage. Shortly afterwards another fire was placed among some shavings under the store of Mr. Posner and blazed to an considerable height. Fortunately it was extinguished without any material damage.[2]

Although no further major problems in connection with the legislature seem to have occurred, Louisville remained a rather rowdy town and many of the citizens seem to have pressed for action. The Board of Commissioners of Louisville, under the direction of Chairman John Shelman and Clerk Peter J. Carnes, drew up an ordinance in 1799 to try to bring order back to the town. This ordinance, which was called "An Ordinance to Prevent Persons from Galloping Horses in the Streets of Louisville and Other Disorderly Behavior," was printed in September of 1799 in the *State Gazette and Louisville Journal*. The ordinance stated that some people were galloping and running their horse in the streets of Louisville and that these actions were dangerous and inconvenient for the inhabitants of Louisville. It also mentioned that people were frequently collecting in the streets and other places and conducting themselves in "a wanton disorderly and riotous manner, which also tends greatly to disturb the tranquility of the said inhabitants."

Because of the problems with rowdy behavior, the commissioners of Louisville passed an ordinance to fine any person "who shall run, gallop, ride or drive in a disorderly manner" in the streets of Louisville. Those people who were guilty of disorderly behavior by "getting intoxicated, and wrangling, fighting, or profane swearing, or in any manner conducting him or themselves, so as to disturb the peace and good order" were not to be fined more than two dollars for the first offence or more than ten dollars for additional offenses. If people could not or would not pay the fines, they were to "be confined in the stocks, imprisoned, or whipped at the discretion of the board or a majority of them." No one, however, was to "receive more than thirty-nine lashes, be committed to the stocks for a longer time than six hours, or be imprisoned longer than the term of thirty days for any of the aforesaid offenses." If these offenses were committed on the Lord's Day, however, the fines or punishment could be doubled.[3]

Some fighting did occur in Louisville, and, at times, some of the public officials were involved in it. In a letter to the editor of the *Louisville Gazette and Republican Trumpet* of 1800, one Godfrey Betsill told about Horation Marbury, a justice of the peace, who, forgetting about his oath to preserve peace, got two old men who were drunk to fight. When they stopped fighting, Marbury tried to force them to fight again. Mr. Betsill and his brother requested that Mr. Marbury not make the old men fight any more since they were already hurt and torn. Marbury then struck Betsill's brother, and when his brother tried to defend himself, Marbury, observed Betsill,

> Slave-like and coward-like, sheltered himself under the cloak of his office, commanded a guard to take us into custody, issued a warrant, and confined my brother and myself in a loatsome [*sic*] jail, until we were berated by a judge of the Inferior Court on a writ of Habeus [*sic*] Corpus, and Marbury's proceedings declared illegal.[4]

Business Activity

As Louisville became the capital of Georgia, it began to experience extensive economic growth. In 1796 the Jefferson County Tax Digest listed three merchants who had general merchandise stores—Joseph G. Posner (with $2,000 of stock), Michael Shellman (with $500 of stock), and Charles Gachett (with $150 of stock). Between 1796 and 1799 Louisville attracted and developed several new businesses. These included the general merchandise stores of Manus Lemle, Ebenezer Jenckes, John Shelman, James Bozeman, William Alexander, John Barron, and David Thomas; the drug business of Pugsley and Deveaux; the shoe business of Daniel McDowell; the tailor businesses of Joseph Stevens, John Housley, and Joseph White; the blacksmith shop of Job Tounsley; and the watch-making and jewelry business of Andrew Burns.[5]

By 1801, nine general merchandise stores were competing for business in Louisville, but many of the earlier merchants had gone out of business. The Louisville merchants of 1801 were James Bozeman, Josiah M. Sterett, Z. Lamar, John Shelman, Charles Gachet, James Meriwether, J. G. Posner, Michael Shelman, and Ebenezer Jenches. Jenches had the largest stock in town, and it was valued at $4,500. Between 1801 and 1804 A. Hammond, J. Sawyer, and David McCormick opened general merchandise businesses; Gregory and Bounticoue opened a clock and watchmaker business; James Willey opened a tailor shop; and Mr. Gobert opened a confectionery store that sold candy, cakes, and medicine.[6]

In 1804 Louisville was at the peak of its prosperity, and nine prosperous merchants were living there. These included Francis McMurray, Z. Lamar, Daniel Lemle, John Shelman, Walter Robinson, Ebenezer Jenckes, Isaac Bower, James Meriwether, and Charles Gachette. Josiah M. Sterett and Joseph Davis also had stores in Louisville in 1804.

Joseph Chairs had a grain mill around Louisville, and Francis Coleman had a grist mill.[7]

In 1806, the Scottish traveler John Melish said:

> There are ten dry-good and grocery stores in the place, and they have a considerable inland trade. Louisville is at present the seat of government, but it is about to be moved to Milledgeville, a new settlement, about 50 miles distant.[8]

Mr. Melish also described the town of Louisville and the area around it. He said that Louisville:

> Consists of about 100 dwelling houses and contains about 550 inhabitants of whom nearly one half are slaves. It is built on an elevated situation, and there is a pretty extensive view to the westward; but considerable effluvia is generated on the banks of the river, which renders the place rather unhealthy. The country and the neighborhood is [sic] well cultivated, and Louisville contains a civil, well bred society.[9]

All of the stores in early Louisville were what are called "general stores," because they stocked almost everything. It is interesting to look at some of the things that these stores advertised for sale to the public. One advertisement included various types of brandy, rum pater, gin molasses, sugar, coffee, chocolate, tea, cinnamon, cloves, nutmeg, mace, allspice, black pepper, writing paper, crockery, prunes, soap, vinegar, cigars, spirits of turpentine, and sweet oil.[10] One should note that goods could be bartered for as well as bought with money.

Aside from spirits and groceries, you could also purchase in the stores of Louisville such things as broadcloths, buff cassimere, dussil blankets, linen, calicoes, muslins, durants, oznaburgs, cotton bagging, plain and colored cotton hose, velvets and thicksets, royal ribb, patent medicine of all kinds, gun locks, bridle bits, plated spurs, women's stirrup irons, hardware of all kinds, pen knives, saddle tacks, cotton cards, ribbons, scissors, ladies hair combs, sewing silk all colors, pocket handkerchiefs, girt webbing, thimbles, neck laces, and razors in cases.[11]

For finer things one could shop at the store of William Alexander where you could purchase silver French watches, tea and salt spoons, silver and plated soup ladles, plated castors and candlesticks, silver bridle furniture, silver clasps and sleeve buttons, silver and plated whips, gold medallions and chains, gold lockets and bosom pins, gold enamel and chased bracelets, gilt medallions and bracelets, gold square and crescent clasps, elegant ladies pocketbooks, gentlemen's pocketbooks, and an elegant assortment of artificial fruit.[12]

To strengthen the economy of their city, the early town fathers of Louisville had a vision of boats going up and down the Ogechee River from Louisville to the Atlantic Ocean carrying loads of cotton and other goods. The business community pushed to make this a reality from 1796 to at least as late as 1816. The first evidence of a desire to make Louisville a port city came from the *House of Representative Journal* of 21 February 1796, which refers to an act "to raise money for the purpose of opening and improving the navigation of Ogeechee River from Louisville to the mouth thereof."[13]

The *House of Representatives Journal* in 1799 also recorded a bill from the Georgia Senate entitled "An Act to Incorporate a Company for the Improvement of the navigation of Ogeechee River, from the mouth of Rocky Comfort Cr. to the mouth of Bird's Mill Creek."[14] In November 1801, the Georgia House of Representatives considered an act "to incorporate a company for the improvement of the navigation of that part of the Ogeechee River between Louisville and Paramour' Bluff."[15]

Apparently the work of the leading citizens of Louisville paid off, because the *Louisville Gazette and Republican Trumpet* of December 1802 contains an announcement that the "Legislature passed an act to establish a lottery for the purpose of improving the navigation of Ogeechee and Canuchee Rivers."[16] Further details of this lottery were given in the April 1803 edition of the same paper. The plan was to sell 7,000 tickets at two dollars each. To get people to buy these tickets, the legislature planned to "give away 2,333 prizes at a cost of $10,500."[17] Through this scheme they hoped to raise $3,000. It is not clear whether or not the tickets sold well or whether the lottery brought in the hoped for money.

Some people, on the other hand, were not convinced that it was worthwhile to make the Ogeechee River navigable. In a letter to the editor in a Louisville newspaper of 1801, the writer questioned clearing the Ogeechee for navigation. He pointed out that some goods have come up the river from Savannah in the past, but he said that "the truth is that the river is too small to be kept completely cleared."[18]

The "Market House" or, as many people call it, the "Old Slave Market" was the site of much of the commercial activity of early Louisville. At this building many different types of sales, including

"Sheriff's Sales," "Coroner's Sales," and "Collector's Sales," took place. Sales for stray animals and land were held there.[19] Slaves also were sold there.[20]

The market house was also the site of public punishment. In one case a Mr. Fuller was "to receive thirty lashes on his bare back, that is to say 10 lashes at the market place in Louisville on the morrow being the 23rd instantee and 20 lashes on Friday the 24th instance between 8 and 10 O'clock and then discharged."[21]

Although some tradition says that the market house was built in 1758 at the convergence of two important Indian trails, no evidence exists to support this tradition. More likely, the market house was erected during the period when Louisville was the state capital and when the town promised to become an important commercial center.[22]

Hanging in the old market house is a bell thought to have been cast in France in 1772. The bell, it is said, was designed for a convent in New Orleans, but the French boat on which the bell was shipped was sacked by pirates. The pirate boat was in turn captured near Savannah, and the bell was retaken and later sent inland to the new state capital.[23]

Louisville's Professionals

Since it was a new town on the frontier, one might think that early Louisville had no professional people other than politicians. Because it was the capital, however, Louisville attracted a number of lawyers and doctors. In the 1796 tax digest, Louisville is listed as having two lawyers: Henry Caldwell and Peter Williamson. The earliest information about physicians also comes from the tax digest, which lists Josiah Sterrett, Thomas Ringland, and Thomas Pugsley as doctors practicing in Louisville.[24] Before 1800, Dr. John Powell joined the Louisville physicians.

Other physicians also joined this group through the years. The Louisville newspaper of March 1801 announced that Dr. Matthew Rowan was going to practice "physic and surgery" in Louisville.[25] Later in 1801, Dr. Schley announced that he was opening up a practice in Louisville.[26]

Dr. Powell's practice apparently became so large that he added a partner. In the June 1804, Dr. Powell notified the people of the area that he had taken Dr. Sayre into copartnership with him in the practice of "Physic and Surgery" and that he had moved his "medicine shop to Mr. Bozeman's storehouse, next door to Col. Shelman's boarding-house."[27]

Most of these doctors seem to have stayed only a few years in Louisville, because in the 1809 tax digest Micaiah H. Powell, Josiah Sterrett, Eli M. A. Corcibzea, and John Powell were the only physicians listed.

The most successful and famous of these physicians was Dr. John Powell. By 1814, he was one of the richest and most influential men in Jefferson County. According to the 1814 tax digest, he owned 63 slaves, 1,936 acres in Jefferson County, 1,019 acres in Burke County, 490 acres in Wayne County, 500 acres in Camden County, 2,300 acres in Franklin County, and a lot worth $1,050 in Louisville.[28]

Dr. Powell played a key role in the visit of the Scottish traveler John Melish when he came to Louisville in July 1806. Melish wrote that he had a very high fever when he arose one morning, and he described how Dr. Powell dealt with him. Powell invited Melish into his house and introduced him to Mrs. Powell. He stayed with them for several days, by which means he "was relieved from the bustle of a public tavern, and still more disagreeable sting of the musquitoes [*sic*] which the bedrooms in it were infested."[29]

Melish visited Louisville again in April of 1810 and returned to see Dr. Powell. He wrote of his second visit:

I found the seat of government had been moved to Milledgeville; but my friend Dr. Powell still remained at this place; and I passed a very agreeable evening with his family. The doctor was not at home, and I regretted much that I had not an opportunity for thanking him for his kindness and attention when I was here before.[3]

Printing and Newspapers

When the capital moved to Louisville, concern began to develop about who would print all of the documents for the state because there were no printing offices in the new town of Louisville.

Beginning in 1796, the legislature met regularly in Louisville, but the journals of the House of Representatives for the session of January and February of 1796 were printed in Augusta by a printing firm owned by John Erdman Smith. Smith was also awarded a $500 contract for printing the legislative journals of 1797, but there was a proviso that he should "establish a press in Louisville on or before 1st October next."[31] Even though a petition was submitted to the legislature for the establishment of a printing office in Louisville on 17 January 1797, no printing company opened in Louisville.[32]

Apparently Smith did not comply with the requirements of the contract, because the laws and journals of the session of January and February of 1798 were printed by Alexander McMillan. No press had been established in Louisville at this time since McMillan had all of the state printing done in Augusta. Later in the year 1798, however, McMillan printed the new *Constitution of the State of Georgia*, which had been adopted on 30 May. On it he put the imprint "Louisville: Printed by A. McMillan, Printer to the State." If McMillan ever had a press in Louisville at all, it was only for a short period, since no interruption in the publication of his newspaper the *Centinel* in Augusta seems to have occurred. Apparently he devised a scheme for printing both in Augusta and Louisville, as can be seen from the imprint made in the acts of the session of January and February of 1799. During this time, McMillan was still "printer to the state," but the acts of the session have an interesting imprint: "Louisville: Printed by Elisha H. Waldo for Alexander McMillan."[33] What seemingly happened is that McMillan sublet the state printing work to Elisha H. Waldo, a printer who had located a small press in Louisville. It is not clear who was awarded the contract for the printing of the 1800 session acts and other state records, but it might have been Elisha Waldo, because he had begun a newspaper in Louisville in November of 1798.

In February 1799, someone submitted a proposal to the Georgia Senate and House of Representatives "that he will establish a press at Louisville which will prevent much deliberation on the subject of printing the laws and journals as he is determined to do that business on the lowest consideration possible."[34] The individual is not named, but it was probably Ambrose Day since he began a new newspaper in Louisville in January of 1799.

Soon after this time the job of "printers of the State" was turned over to Ambrose Day and James Hely, the editors of the *Louisville Gazette and Republican Trumpet*. This printing establishment had the state printing contract from 1801 to 1807, and quite possibly had acquired it in 1800. The *House Journal* of 1800 notes that it was printed by "Ambrose Day and James Hely—Printers of the State."[35] With this printing company, the state at last had official printers in Louisville. This company would continue to serve the state until the capital moved to Milledgeville.

In 1798, one printer became brave enough to begin a newspaper in Louisville. Elisha H. Waldo set up a printing office on Eighth Street and printed the first issue of his paper, the *State Gazette and Louisville Journal* on 27 November 1798. If the existing copies can be taken as typical, this paper was little more than an official bulletin with the addition of some state, national and international miscellany. He informed his patrons that in his office "printing in all its variety executed with neatness and dispatch." The paper was printed every Wednesday and sold for $3.00 annually.[36]

What happened to the *State Gazette and Louisville Journal* is not clear, but only a few issues from the last two months of 1798 still exist. Whatever may have been the reason, a new newspaper came into existence during the early days of 1799, so it is quite probable that Mr. Waldo's press was sold or put into operation for this new paper.

The new paper was called the *Louisville Gazette*, and it was edited by Ambrose Day. On 22 January 1799, the first issue of the paper was printed. In this issue, Mr. Day clearly pointed out that this paper would "ever be open to all parties—influenced by none." He promised to adhere to the strictest impartiality and to make it into " a useful and entertaining paper."[37]

In 1800, this newspaper added James Hely as a partner and changed its name to the *Louisville Gazette and Republican Trumpet*.[38] This partnership between Day and Hely lasted until the beginning of 1805, when Ambrose Day announced that the partnership had been dissolved and that he would now run the paper by himself.[39] The *Louisville Gazette and Republican Trumpet* remained under the direction of Ambrose Day until 1811, but the name was changed back to the *Louisville Gazette* in 1810.[40]

During 1801, James Mylie opened a printing office on Seventh street and published the *Independent Register* as a competitor to the *Louisville Gazette and Republican Trumpet*. Apparently his venture was not very successful, and his newspaper disappeared from the scene.

Almost all of the early newspapers of Louisville were four printed pages, usually having four columns on each page. The greater percent of the space in these papers was devoted to legal notices, wanted notices, and advertisements. A fair amount of space was also used to discuss the domestic news from Boston and Philadelphia, and it included an extensive amount of foreign news from such exotic places as Paris, Vienna, and London. The pages in all of these early Louisville newspapers, however, included almost no news from Georgia or the local area. In addition, the papers had many advertisements for land sales, and once every month it contained a notice about who had not picked up their mail at the post office. The newspaper frequently included election results and interesting things about the weather. Poems, essays, and other literary works were also regularly included in these newspapers.

The only early newspaper really to take hold, the *Louisville Gazette*, which later became the *Louisville Gazette and Republican Trumpet*, found it very difficult to stay alive financially. The demise of the printer is clearly seen in an article that Ambrose Day put in his paper on 17 December 1799. He wrote:

> Subscribers who are indebted for the *Louisville Gazette* or for any other printing done at this office, are requested to come forward and pay up their arrears. . . . The great expenses incident to an establishment such as a newspaper, ought to be impressed on the minds of the subscribers, and induce them to discharge the amount of their accounts with greater punctuality. The Editor can certainly say that, in establishing the *Louisville Gazette*, he was actuated more by a desire to comply with the numerous solicitations of gentlemen in several parts of the state, and a hope of its proving advantageous to the country, than by any prospect of gain to himself; the expenses of the business have hitherto very far exceeded the receipts from it.[41]

In May 1804, the editors of the *Louisville Gazette and Republican Trumpet* printed a notice that the newspaper "has urgent need for payment of debts."[42] Apparently things were not going well for the newspaper so a month later a note appeared that the newspaper "removed to dwelling house occupied by editors."[43]

With numerous peoples not paying their accounts and charges of only $3.00 a year for the newspaper, it is understandable why the Louisville newspapers were continuously looking for ways to supplement their revenues. One typical way was to sell advertisements, and this was done on a limited scale. How many advertisements could someone sell in a small town like Louisville? Some issues of the papers contained virtually no advertisements, so little revenue was gained through this means.

At the Louisville newspaper office one could get many types of printing done and could purchase pencils, camphorated sealing wax, the best black ink, and other writing supplies, as well as blank deeds and blank collector's titles.[44]

In addition to this, the printing office also acted as the local employment and trading office. You could inquire about a young man "who had been accustomed to attend in a Dry Good or Grocery Store"; a black woman "who can cook, wash, and iron"; "an apprentice to the bricklayers trade"; a "convenient store"; a "valuable tenement"; or a pair of oxen at the newspaper office.[45]

The newspapers also sold subscriptions to many types of publications, as well as a full length portrait of Thomas Jefferson and copies of General Washington's will. One could likewise buy music books for the violin, harpsichord, guitar, flute, clarinet, and hautboy, and even a real German flute. Also, one could buy there lottery tickets for "the improvement of navigation of the Ogeechee and Canouchi Rivers."[46]

At times the newspaper office was even a jewelry store. In 1799 the *Louisville Gazette* placed an advertisement that it had for sale gold earrings, gold wares, gift seals "to tell the day and the month," silver bottle ladles, silver boot buckles, plated spurs, and plated whips, as well as needles, buttons, shaving soap, muslin handkerchiefs, and many other fine things.[47]

Another way of earning money for the newspaper and at the same time providing a valuable community service was its function as the local bookstore. At the newspaper office one could purchase "cheap for cash" a real variety of books, including such titles as *"Brookes's Gazetteer, History of the Heavens, Hargraves Law Tracts, History of Paraguay, Gordons's Tacitus, Spencer's Works, Gulliver's Travels, Brissot on Commerce, Haunted Priory, Franklin's Life, Elements of Fortification, Constitutions of the United States, Nihell on the Pulse, American Accountant, Wilson's Arithmetic, Complete French Master for Ladies and Gentlemen, An Introduction to Geography, Select Plays, Calvinism Improved, A Hieroglyphical Bible, A Defence of the Old Testament, A Dictionary of Love,* and many other titles. The newspaper office also sold Greek and Latin school books, French and Dutch books, merchant account books, children's books, receipt books, and writing equipment.[48]

One can see from this list that the people of Louisville were given the opportunity to buy books of high quality and variety. This indicates the intellectual level of the people living there in the 1800s. This valuable service to the community of Louisville and Jefferson County was just another method that the local newspaper used to keep itself alive financially.

Even when the newspapers were in good shape financially, they frequently ran into trouble because of some of the things they printed. Sometimes they were attacked. At least one incident occurred in which one of the newspapers was actually sued. A real attack came on the newspaper office in September of 1800, which is fully recorded in the *Louisville Gazette and Republican Trumpet*. The newspaper reported the event as follows:

> Last evening about the hour of 10 o'clock, the following persons collected to wit: John Berrien, extreasurer of this State, John M. Berrien, his son, Col. John Cobbs, with his two sons, Capt. Robert Flournoy, Dr. John Pugsley and several other persons came to our printing office, and knocked at the door, and were answered from within, who is there? They made no answer but knocked again: we not suspecting any mischief opened the door when the above named persons rushed in armed with clubs and whips—John Cobbs who appeared to be the leader of the party asked if there were any pieces for publication; he was answered, yes: he then lifted a whip, was aiming at Ambrose Day, one of his own party stopped him: he afterwards made at Jas. Hely and swore that he was the one he was at—when the noise brought a concourse of citizens to the place; they were then obliged to desist. We have since applied to the civil magistrates who have given us their words they shall be bound over to keep the peace. The above persons have been loud brawlers for several years past in favor of regular government of which the above assassinous attack may be taken as a specimen.[49]

Although the problems with the Louisville brawlers made the newspaper look like a hero, in one situation the Louisville newspaper did not look so good. For some reason, a big feud erupted between the editors of the *Louisville Gazette and Republican Trumpet* and William J. Hobby, the editor of the *Augusta Herald*. This feud began as early as 1800 and lasted at least until 1803. The attacks from both sides were rather frequent and became so vicious that William J. Hobby sued Ambrose Day and James Hely for "false and malicious libel." A Savannah newspaper of May 1803 told about this case and mentioned that it came up in Federal Circuit Court where Hobby won and was awarded $2,000 in damages.[50]

In the early days of Louisville, libel and slander seem to have been rather unknown concepts in the newspaper. People could make virtually any statement they wanted and not worry about backing it up with any evidence. If one was unhappy with some businessman or with his wife, he could put it in the newspaper for the whole community to read.

One such article appeared in the *Louisville Gazette and Republican Trumpet* of June 1803. It read:

> Richard Berry forewarns all gentlemen from admitting Joseph P. Slade, watch cobler, into their company on any pretence whatever, as he is not worthy of their confidence. He has lately taken the benefit of the gambling act, in violation of all the rules of that honorable profession.[51]

Joseph P. Slade responded to this article written by Richard Berry as follows:

> Having propagated several reports injurious to my character and reputation, and in addition to many insults, has forewarned all gentlemen against receiving me into their company. Although it is a doubt with me whether gentle or simple will pay any attention to his metrical valedictory that appeard last Wednesday—yet I deem it a duty incumbent upon me, to refute his scandalous affirmation. Berry's sudden departure from this place has deprived me of an opportunity of calling him personally to an account.[52]

In the newspaper of March 1803 Wm. Thompson of Louisville announced to the public that John Holland of Savannah was "a snake in the grass, a poltroon, a jerry sneak, a rascal, and an arrant coward."[53]

It was more common for a man to criticize his wife and refuse to pay any debts that she incurred. John Dunn gave the following notice:

> Whereas my wife Ann, has absconded from my bed and board, for some time; without any lawful cause, I do hereby forewarn all persons whatsoever, from trading with her, harbouring her or paying her any money due to me, either by bond, note, or book account, as I will not be answerable for any of her dealings, nor pay any contracts she makes."[54]

Another similar article appeared in the same Louisville newspaper as James McDonald gave notice that

> my wife, Esther, from causes unknown, is fallen into a state of insanity: and as there are many people in the world who would wish to take the[sic] advantage of me and to trust her for all such articles, which her

foolish fancy may covet. I do therefore forewarn all persons from dealing with her, as I will not be answerable for any of her contracts.[55]

Entertainment in Early Louisville

In addition to reading the newspapers, people in early Louisville found many ways to keep themselves entertained, some of which were quite sophisticated.

One of the major forms of entertainment was a visit to the "Coffee House" where there were "accomodations for gentlemen during the sitting of the Legislature and through the winter season." This entertainment was composed of much conversation and a greater amount of drinking.[56]

Also meeting weekly in early Louisville at the "Coffee House" was the Union Society, an evening intellectual debating club that discussed such topics as: "What qualifications ought a representative of the people to possess?" "Whether the federal system in its present operation is or is not best for the welfare of the U.S?" "Whether or not the culture of cotton or tobacco is the most advantageous to the State of Georgia?"[57]

A description of one of the Union Society meetings is given in a letter to the editor by "A Friend to Debating Societies," who said "curiosity induced me to pay them a visit." When he came, he "found a number of patriotic speakers, men of good talents, capable of discussing subjects of the highest importance." To his astonishments, he found them to "lay aside important questions to give way for little insignificant ones, about Irish Potatoes." He notes, however, that several of the best orators and most patriotic members were not there that evening. He concluded by saying, "If after this I find them publish some good questions, I should be highly gratified to become a member and would give my feeble support to so excellent an institution." Thus, intellectual entertainment and stimulation existed in early Louisville, as well as that of a more common nature.[58]

Louisville, since it was the capital, became a center for entertainment, and it attracted a variety of traveling shows. In 1799, Louisville was visited by the "Learned Pig," and the citizens were offered the opportunity of "gratifying their curiosity, as the pig will leave town soon."[59] In 1800, the "famous double-headed rattle snake" came to visit. For those who wished "to penetrate into this mysterious and stupendous sport of nature" they were given the opportunity to observe him through a magnifying glass. The price to see this strange creature was twelve and a half cents.[60]

Even more sophisticated entertainment arrived in Louisville in 1801. At this time a group called the "Rope Dancers" came to town and put on performances at the courthouse. This act included wire dancing and tumbling. As an added attraction, the show included a naval scene, consisting, in part, of American Navy and French ships of war, "which will come to action and display several of the events which lately took place between the Constellation and the French frigate La Vengeance."[61]

Another interesting performance took place in Louisville in 1802 when a Mr. Johnson went to "considerable expense in building a temporary circus, for the purpose of giving one or two elegant representations of the noble art of horsemanship."[62]

Louisville even had a "large and elegant exhibition of Waxwork" to come to town in 1803. This attraction was housed in the home of Mr. John Shelman and consisted of such interesting figures as Thomas Jefferson, George Washington, John Adams, Bonaparte, Dr. Ezra Stiles, the late president of Yale College, and an Indian chief with a tomahawk and scalping knife in his hands. One could carefully observe all of these fine figures while "music on an elegant organ" played in the background.[63]

Fun and entertainment were especially enjoyed on certain important days such as St. Patrick's Day and Independence Day. In 1803 the whole of Louisville celebrated St. Patrick's Day at the home of John Downer. As the major part of the celebration, the people drank the following toasts with a musical accompaniment:

> Immortal memory of St. Patrick; the land of potatoes with its sons and daughters all over the world and in the USA; Thomas Jefferson, the President; the memory of General Washington; James Monroe; the State of Georgia; our representatives in congress; the memory of George Galphin, our revered countryman whose virtues require no panegyric; public good; republics; dead and surviving of the Revolutionary War; the Irish Patriots; General Wilkinson; Fair Daughters of America; etc.[64]

The most important of all festivities was held on the Fourth of July. The activities lasted all day, beginning in the early morning with the militia firing a "federal salute" and continuing throughout the day with "sham fights." After these sham fights, the eating and drinking began. The Louisville newspaper described the day as being spent in a "happy and social manner, which ever characterizes true republicans."[65]

The Scottish traveler John Melish gave an interesting account of his 4 July 1806 experiences in Louisville:

> This being the anniversary of American independence, the day was ushered in by the firing of great guns; and military companies had collected in Louisville from the whole country around. On my return to the cabin, I found a considerable number of the military assembled there. I was waited on by a committee of the artillery company and received a very polite invitation to dine with them, which I accepted with pleasure, being anxious to observe the mode of celebrating the day, so important in the annals of America. . . . After dinner they drank Mederia wine to a series of toasts. Each toast was followed by a discharge of artillery, and the music played an appropriate air. A number of excellent songs were sung, and the afternoon was spent with great conviviality and good humor. Having several calls to make in the town, I left the table early, but returned again in the evening, when I found that the 'cordial drop' had added greatly to the elevation of the animal spirits of the company.[66]

His experiences in Louisville caused Melish to make the following statements: "The whole of my observations in this place tended to convince me that the American character is very indifferently understood in Britain and indeed very much misrepresented."[67]

It is clear that the people of Louisville liked to have fun and be entertained, and they took advantage of every opportunity to enjoy themselves. But there was also a more serious side to them and this can be seen in their religious life.

Religious Life

Before the capital came to Louisville, the religious needs of people were filled by churches and by meetings held in the area of Jefferson County. Several Presbyterian churches, as has already been mentioned, were established in the Jefferson County area between 1780 and 1790. Apparently a church was located at Ebenezer, which had earlier been called Fleeting Meeting House, and another at Bethel, both of which were near modern Vidette, as well as a church at Queensborough. The same minister was the pastor of all three. The Indians and the English did great harm to these churches during the Revolutionary War, but they survived, albeit with less strength than before. David Bothwell, from Ireland, became pastor of these churches in 1790, beginning a revitalization of these congregations. This clergyman had become widely known and highly respected before he died at the home of Governor Jared Irwin in 1801.[68]

In addition to the problems caused by the Revolutionary War, the Presbyterian churches in the area experienced a great deal of competition from the Baptist and Methodist churches that began to spring up all over the Georgia frontier.

The first Baptist church in Jefferson County was Providence, which began in 1785 on Rocky Comfort Creek some twelve miles west of Louisville. It was originally called Vining's Meeting Place after the Reverend Jethro Vining, who was instrumental in organizing the church. Some of the early pastors were John Newton, Thomas Mercer, Norvell Robertson, and Benjamin Davis[69]

Old Bethel Baptist Church on Rocky Creek was constituted on 9 May 1795 with some help from the Providence Church. It began with fifteen members, but by 1804 the membership had increased to sixty.[70]

Louisville was established as a new town on the frontier and tended to attract some rather rough and irreligious people. With the arrival of the governor and the legislature in 1796, Louisville took on a somewhat more religious flavor, but still it was far from being a "religious town." Although several churches had been established in the rural areas around Louisville, no church stood in the town of Louisville until 1811. Finally, a church building was constructed, but not for a specific church. The building was open for any denomination that wished to use it.

The fact that no church existed in Louisville did not mean that the town had no religious people. On 11 February 1796, "sundry persons inhabitants of Louisville and the vicinity" petitioned the Georgia legislature to give financial assistance to this group so that they would be able to support a minister.[71] Apparently no help was given because no full-time or part-time minister came during this time.

One of the presentments of the Jefferson County Grand Jury of 1799 was about "the little regard which is paid to the religious observance of the Lord's day."[72] The grand jury presentments of 1802 included one concerning the fact that the "law prohibiting profane swearing is not better executed," and two others concerning couples who were living in adultery.[73] Clearly, people in Louisville and Jefferson County were religious and concerned about morality even though there were few churches in the county and none in Louisville.

The major part of Louisville's worship, and perhaps the only worship, was done at the state house. Numerous itinerant preachers of all denominations and a few of the local ministers came to the state house. After reserving the building for their services, the ministers, hoping to have a sizeable audience, would advertise their meeting in the local newspaper. The most frequent speaker at the state house was the Reverend David Bothwell.[74] Other speakers included Rector Thomas Carter; Phillips Gibbes;[75] Rev. Stith Mead;[76] Rev. Mr. Hull of Augusta;[77] and Rev. M. L. Weems, rector of Mt. Vernon Parish Virginia in Virginia.[78]

One religious advertisement of January 1800 stated, "As there is no preaching, nor divine worship in this place, all those who wish to attend at the State House on the next Sunday will hear a sermon and church prayers read by me, William Goold."[79] Other newspaper advertisements show that religious services were taking place all around Louisville. The Reverend Hope Hull notified the public in 1803 that he and several other preachers would be preaching in "Louisville on Thursday 14th of July and at Old Town on Friday, Saturday and Sunday."[80] It is not clear why Reverend Hull was to spend only one day preaching in Georgia's capital while he spent three days in Old Town. An advertisement in 1804 told of ten or twelve preachers coming to Bethel, which is about nine miles above Louisville "in order to preach, pray, and exercise other religious duties for four or five days."[81]

One should note that Bishop Francis Asbury, who is called the "Father of Methodism in America," preached at Galphin's Old Town where "the house was open, and the day was cold" on 2 March 1790.[82] On 28 January 1803, he passed through Louisville and stopped at the home of Mr. Flournoy, "a new convert whose wife was amongst the respectables." He also preached at a new chapel in the woods of Jefferson County called Bethel on 30 January 1803.[83]

Although most of the itinerant ministers found Louisville an excellent place to visit and preach the gospel, one Lorenza Dow, a rather eccentric Methodist minister who had traveled throughout the United States, did not find it so. In his journal of November 1803, Dow wrote that he spoke to "as many as could conveniently get into the statehouse." Apparently his message was not well received by everyone because while he was speaking, Lorenza noted, "I perceived the chair in which I stood on the writing table to move twice or thrice because of which I could not then ascertain but sat down to prevent my falling."[84]

After the meeting, a young man explained to Reverend Dow that a Baptist minister had put his foot on the chair several times, apparently with the desire to turn Dow over and bring laughter to the audience. This rivalry between Methodists and Baptists in early Georgia took on a rather comical atmosphere when the young man went to the Baptist minister and threatened him with his fist because of his actions toward Rev. Dow.

Unfortunately for the young man, the Baptist minister was also a Georgia legislator. He complained to the legislature about being insulted. The legislature then ordered the young man to go to prison and the next day to trial because no legislator could be insulted while he was sitting in the legislature. The young man pleaded that the man was not in a legislative session at the time, and so he was acquitted.

Apparently the legislature, and in particular the governor, were rather embarrassed by the whole episode and tried to smooth the situation over by sending to Lorenza Dow a "recommendation as a preacher of the gospel to the world of mankind, signed by the Governor, Secretary and 28 members of the Legislature with the great seal of the State."[85]

The University of Georgia in Louisville?

In addition to religion, education was an important matter to the people of Louisville and Jefferson County. When the Georgia legislature drew up the law for the establishment of Louisville as the "seat of government," they included a section stating that the commissioners of Louisville should reserve land not only for the state house and other public buildings but also for the "University."[86] At this time it was the assumption that the university would be located in the same place. Why this 1786 ruling was never carried out is not completely clear. Even as late as February 1796 a Mr. Cobb notified the House of Representatives that he would move for a committee "to establish a college in the town of Louisville."[87]

The Georgia Assembly, on 27 January 1785, granted a charter for the University of Georgia and also set up a "Board of Trustees" and a "Board of Visitors," which together were called the "Senatus Academicus." They were to be the governing body for the university and were to meet annually.[88]

In 1789, the state adopted a new constitution that did away with some official positions and added another house (the Senate) to the general assembly. This action eliminated some of the members of the

Board of Visitors and Senatus Academicus and made it impossible for them to meet legally.

With all of this confusion and the impossibility of holding a legal meeting of the Senatus Academicus, it is not surprising that the first meeting of this body, of which no record remains, did not take place until fourteen years after it had been authorized. According to the *Executive Department Minutes* of 6 March 1797, the secretary of the state was ordered to prepare a proclamation "notifying and requiring" a meeting of the Senatus Academicus at Louisville on 10 July 1797.[89] This group did not meet, but a resolution was circulated and signed by seven trustees of the university filling six vacancies and calling for a meeting to be held on 1 July 1798.

On 2 July 1798, four trustees appeared in Louisville, but since a quorum was not present, they adjourned to the next day, when seven members appeared. For the following two days the trustees were in session, and on the last day, they reported that they had on hand $7,463.75, which they considered "sufficiently respectable to commence the building of the University." Taking on life at last, they now called an important meeting to be held at Louisville in early January of 1799.[90]

On 8 January 1799, at the appointed time, some trustees met in Louisville, but no quorum was present until 10 January. Realizing that changes in the state constitution had made it impossible for the Senatus Academicus to function, they suggested on 12 January that the governor, the judges of the superior courts, the president of the Senate, and the Speaker of the House ought to constitute the board of visitors, and they resolved that the legislature be asked to pass "an explanatory act which will obviate all difficulties."

On 15 February 1799, the governor issued a proclamation requiring the Senatus Academicus of the University of Georgia "to convene at Louisville between the terms of the superior courts in the present year, to take under consideration, and adopt such measures as may best promote the object of that institution."[91]

The first real meeting of the Senatus Academicus took place in Louisville in November of 1799. Even then, the meeting was not a legal one, for it was not until the next year that the legislature, in the Act of 1800, made possible the formation of a legal board of visitors and consequently an official Senatus Academicus. The *Louisville Gazette* of December 1799 noted that the Senatus Academicus met and "appointed Judge Carnes, Judge Mitchell, and Mr. Clay, a committee to confer with the trustees of the different academies in the state about funds, tutors, pupils, salaries and buildings for a university."[92]

On the last two days of this meeting (30 November and 2 December 1799) the Senatus Academicus busied itself with trying to settle on a "temporary site of the University." It assumed that one of the county academies might afford such a site. It considered five such academies (of Columbia, Hancock, Wilkes, Greene, and Jefferson counties), but none was acceptable to the majority. The next day, the vote was taken again but with no decision. They now decided to postpone any further consideration until their next meeting the following year, and in the meantime to send out a letter to all the county academies in the state, asking for a statement of their funds and endowments.[93]

The *Georgia Gazette* announced in July of 1800 that the Senatus Academicus would be meeting in Louisville on the fourth Monday in November of 1800.[94] When the Senatus Academicus convened, it found reports from eight academies. It took up the matter of choosing a site for building a "wing of the University," indicating that it was to be a permanent location. In the meantime, the Senatus Academicus seems to have forgotten that the Act of 1786 had designated Louisville as the site of the university. More probably, that law was considered obsolete since fourteen years had elapsed. Motions were successively made to locate the "wing" in Greene, Franklin, Hancock, and Jackson counties. Greene was agreed upon, and a committee was appointed to build a wing of the university there that would accommodate one hundred students.

On 5 December 1800, the legislature passed an act that amended the charter of the university by adding to the board of visitors all the senators except those from the counties that were otherwise represented in the Senatus Academicus. This act also named thirteen trustees, all of whom were new except Abraham Baldwin, and deprived them of the old charter provision of self-perpetuation. Most importantly for this book, the legislature officially withdrew the site of the university from Louisville.

Undoubtedly political considerations were running riot in the attempt to choose a site for the university. The legislature in its Act of 1800, ignoring the fact that the Senatus Academicus had already chosen Greene, listed the counties in which the university might be located: Jackson, Franklin, Hancock, Greene, Oglethorpe, Wilkes, and Warren. On 16 June 1801, the Senatus Academicus met again in Louisville. It reconsidered the choice of Greene County as "the permanent site of the University." After several votes, the choice soon narrowed to Hancock and Jackson, with the latter finally winning eleven to ten on the seventh ballot.[95]

A Louisville newspaper of June 1801 announced that the Senatus Academicus of the university would meet in Louisville on the first Wednesday of November in 1801.[96] Apparently at this or some other meeting during that year, the location of the university was finally decided when Governor John Milledge gave the University of Georgia trustees 630 acres of land in Athens, on which the university was to be built. Professor, later President, Josiah Meigs, arrived at the site of Athens in 1801 and began to erect the university in that backwoods area of Georgia.[97]

Although Louisville was not to be the home of the University of Georgia, it was in Louisville that many of the decisions about the early days of this university took place. Louisville played a very important role in the location and the beginning of the University of Georgia.

The Academy and Cultural Schools

Even though Louisville was not to have the university, it was to have one of the first academies in Georgia. On 10 February 1799, a Mr. Cobb proposed that a committee be appointed to draw up a bill entitled "An Act to Establish an Academy in the Town of Louisville."[98] This bill met with favor on the part of the legislature and was passed on 22 February 1796.[99] This academy and the academies already erected in Augusta, Waynesbrough, Savannah, Brunswick, and Sunbury were the only ones that had been incorporated in Georgia before the nineteenth century began.[100] It should be noted that the name of this academy in the beginning was really "Jefferson Academy" because all of the state academies were given county names. Because it was located in Louisville, the documents of this early period sometimes called it the "Academy in Louisville" or "Louisville Academy."

The academy in Louisville was one of a group established about that time by the legislature as feeder schools for the state university.[101] The legislature provided for an academy in each county of the state of Georgia to be supported from the same funds and considered as parts and members of the same overall institution.[102]

The first thing this law did was to appoint five influential men from Louisville and Jefferson County to serve as "Commissioners" of this new academy. The men appointed to this position were Rev. David Bothwell,

John Shellman, James Meriwether, John Cobb, and Josiah Sterrett. John Cobb resigned as one of the commissioners in 1797, and Dr. John Powell was appointed in his place. The term of Dr. Powell expired in 1798, and John Berrien was appointed in his place.[103]

In appointing Mr. Berrien, apparently the Georgia legislature failed to take the proper actions to make his appointment legal. He began to function as a commissioner in 1798, however, as if he had been legally placed in that position. This was discovered in 1800, and a scandal broke out. Someone wrote an anonymous letter to the editor of the *Louisville Gazette and Republican Trumpet* in 1800 telling about the illegalities of Mr. Berrien's appointment. The writer said that Berrien was "no more a Commissioner of Jefferson Academy, than the Grand Turk." The community was cautioned that those who had purchased lots from the commissioners should

> look to their deeds of conveyance; such foresight may save their children, and their children's children a long and unnecessary law suit—for the name of John Berrien, as a commissioner at the foot of one of these titles, is of no more consequence than any other cypher.[104]

The law empowered these commissioners to "lay out forty acres of land reserved for the said academy," which belonged to the town of Louisville, "into four acre lots, and also one acre lot for erecting the said academy on." The commissioners were also authorized to sell the lots to the highest bidder and to use this money for the new academy.[105]

Regretfully, a major controversy arose between the commissioners of the academy and the commissioners of the town of Louisville over the land that was to be given by the town to the academy. Apparently, the issue could not be resolved, so the Georgia House of Representatives ordered the commissioners of Louisville "to lay out 41 acres of the town common of Louisville not deranging the plan of the said town now existing in such manner as the Commissioners of the academy may direct."[106]

Realizing that the money from the sale of lots would not really be enough to get the new academy going, the Georgia legislature also included in this law the provision for the commissioners "to purchase confiscated property to the amount of one thousand Pounds," and then to sell it for the use of the academy in Louisville.[107] This confiscated property came from people who supported the British side during the Revolutionary War. The state of Georgia seized it after the war and used the money from its sale to establish academies and other needed things in the state. The legislature later helped the academy by allowing the sale of lots, alleys, and the commons in Louisville.[108]

In addition, the law directed the commissioners that as soon as they raised enough funds they should "erect on said one acre lot, that shall be laid out on the most eligible place and convenient situation for that purpose, a building commodious and proper to answer the intention of this act."[109]

The actual construction of the academy proceeded very slowly. According to Mrs. Smith's notebook, it was seven years before a permanent building was completed for the academy in Louisville. Thus, for almost the entire period that Louisville was the capital, the children of the governor and other state dignitaries were taught in rented quarters with make-shift equipment. The first building was completed in 1803 in the same style as the state house, severely plain with a cupola for a bell. It was a two-story building of brick and plaster with a central doorway flanked by two windows on either side.[110] The school must have been fairly centrally located, probably between Sixth Street, which was the main approach to the capitol, and First Street, which ran along the Ogeechee River and Rocky Comfort Creek. Furnishings were scanty—a teacher's desk, rough benches, and a few writing desks for the more advanced pupils.[111]

Even when the building was finished, the opening was delayed because they had trouble finding someone to be the director of the school. This situation changed in May of 1800, when the commissioners announced "with pleasure, that the Jefferson Academy is now open for the reception of youths, under the direction of Mr. James Armour, from whose character and abilities as a teacher, the Commissioners have great expectations." This school would teach reading, writing, and arithmetic for "three dollars per quarter"; mathematics in all its branches for "four dollars per quarter"; and Latin and Greek languages for "six dollars per quarter."[112]

The problems of getting a director for the academy were not over. In May of 1802 the community was notified that the academy would open under the direction of a new leader, Mr. Truman Hillyer. Apparently they had had trouble getting a full-time person for this position, because in the same notification it added: "Mr. Hillyer would also inform the public, that he will continue his practice of the Law, in the county of Jefferson, and the vacations will be permitted in the Academy during the sessions of court, in said county."[113]

The arrangement with Mr. Hillyer did not last very long, and in August of 1804 the academy advertized "a vacancy in the rectorship of said academy having taken place, a gentleman of good moral character, capable of teaching reading, writing, arithmetic, English grammar, and the Latin and Greek Languages, will meet with encouragement."[114]

Again in 1806, the commissioners of the academy announced that they had engaged a new person, Rev. James L. Wilson, as "rector" of the academy, and that it would open on Monday "the 7th day of July: for the admission of students."[115]

When people think about education in early Louisville, attention always focuses on the academy of Louisville, but few people realize that Louisville was such a "cultured" town that it attracted numerous teachers who wanted to set up their own schools there. A number of teachers came to Louisville trying to compete with the academy, and others tried to add elements that the academy did not teach. One gets a very good picture of these schools from the early Louisville newspapers.

In the *Louisville Gazette* of January 1799, Mr. Andrew Burns placed an advertisement notifying Louisville and the surrounding areas "that he purposes teaching a school in Louisville, providing he meets with encouragement." He planned to teach reading, writing, arithmetic, geometry, trigonometry, surveying, navigation, astronomy, and philosophy for "twelve dollars per annum or one dollar per month."[116]

The general education program suggested by Mr. Burns was copied by several other teachers who wanted to start schools in Louisville. John Barron announced his plans to open a school for the teaching of reading, writing, and arithmetic.[117] The educational opportunities of Louisville even attracted teachers from Augusta, because Mrs. Arthur of that city notified the people of Louisville that she was "desirous of opening a reading school for the education of small boys and girls, the latter of whom she will instruct in needle work."[118] Also in 1799 R. Stone announced his intention to teach an English school.[119]

Other schools also attempted to supplement what was being taught at the academy. In the *Louisville Gazette*, William Keeling placed an advertisement for people "to attend at the State House, in Louisville, in order to open a singing school."[120] Several advertisements appear in the Louisville newspapers from 1799 to 1802 about dancing schools. A Mr. Francis of Augusta tried to start a dancing school in 1799 and was still advertizing his school in 1801,[121] so he must have met with some success. In 1801, Edward Cadusch also tried to start a dancing school, as well as a school that taught other cultural activities such as fencing and the playing of the violin and piano.[122] Apparently, Mr. Cadusch did not attract a large number of students from this advertisement, so in July of the same year, he announced that he "would be glad to find a place in a private family to teach a few scholars the French language—music, vocal and instrumental, and dancing."[123] A Mr. Coleman likewise announced that he would commence a "Dancing School" in September of 1802.[124]

"Those glorious days" brought so many exciting things to the daily life of Louisville and Jefferson County. The presence of the capital in Louisville tremendously influenced the business, cultural, educational, and religious life of this community. With the departure of the capital to Milledgeville, all of this was to change.

Notes

[1]*Executive Department Minutes*, 6 January 1797, 50.

[2]*Columbian Museum and Savannah Advertiser* 13 January 1799.

[3]*State Gazette and Louisville Journal* 3 September 1799. Hereafter this will be abbreviated to *SGLJ*.

[4]*LGRT*, 3 June 1800.

[5]*Jefferson County Tax Digest*, 1796; *LG,* 14 May 1799; *LG,* 22 January 1799; *SGLJ,* 10 December 1799; *LGRT,* 30 September 1800; *LGRT,* 28 October 1800; *LGRT,* 17 December 1800; *LG,* 25 June 1799; *LG,* 17 December 1799; *LG,* 30 June 1799.

[6]*Jefferson County Tax Digest*, 1801; *LGRT,* 10 February 1802; *LGRT,* 4 April 1801; *LGRT,* 20 June 1801; *LGRT,* 10 March 1802.

[7]*Jefferson County Tax Digest*, 1804; *LGRT,* 30 May 1804; *LGRT,* 28 March 1804; *LGRT,* 25 April 1804; *LGRT,* 27 April 1803.

[8]Melish, *Travels*, 39-46.   [9]Ibid., 39-46.

[10]*LG*, 5 November 1799.

[11]*LG*, 26 December 1799.

[12]*LGRT*, 28 October 1800.

[13]*House of Representatives Journal*, 21 February 1796, 149.

[14]Ibid., 4 December 1799, 47.

[15]Ibid., 5 November 1801, 54.

[16]*LGRT*, 1 December 1802.

[17]*LGRT*, 20 April 1803.

[18]*LGRT*, 28 November 1801.

[19]*LG*, 26 January 1799; *LG,* 22 January 1799.

[20]*SGLJ*, 3 September 1799.

[21]*Circut Court Minutes*, 1778 to 1806.

[22]MSS—Milner, 3/10/38, in the University of Georgia Special Collections.

[23]Price, "Louisville," 34.

[24]*Jefferson County Tax Digest*, 1796.

[25]*LGRT*, 7 March 1801.

[26]*LGRT*, 14 November 1801.

[27]*LGRT*, 20 June 1804.

[28]*Jefferson County Tax Digest*, 1814.

[29]Melish, *Travels*, 1:39-46.   [30]Ibid., 374.

[31]D. C. McMurtrie, "Pioneer Printing in Georgia," *Georgia Historical Quarterly* 16/2 (June 1932): 111.

[32]*House of Representatives Journal*, 17 January 1797, 195.

[33]Louis Turner Griffith and John Erwin Talmadge, *Georgia Journalism 1763-1950* (Athens: University of Georgia Press, 1951) 16-17; McMurtrie, "Pioneer Printing in Georgia," 112.

[34]*Governor's Letter Book*, 13 February 1799.

[35]*House of Representatives Journal*, 1801, 66.

[36]*SGLJ*, 30 December 1801.

[37]LG, 22 January 1799.

[38]*LGRT*, 29 April 1800.

[39]*LGRT*, 18 January 1805.

[40]*LG*, 14 May 1810.

[41]*LG*, 17 December 1799.

[42]*LGRT,* 30 May 1804.

[43]*LGRT*, 20 June 1804.

[44]*LG*, 12 March 1799, *LGRT*, 23 April 1800.

[45]*LG*, 22 January 1799; *LGRT*, 20 January 1802; *LGRT*, 10 October 1801; *LGRT*, 13 June 1801; *LGRT*, 15 July 1800; *LGRT*, 14 February 1801.

[46]*LGRT*, 14 November 1801; *LGRT*, 11 April 1801; *LG*, 14 January 1800; *LG*, 2 July 1799; *LGRT*, 7 February 1801; *LGRT*, 29 April 1800; *LGRT*, 14 November 1801; *LGRT*, 20 April 1803.

[47]*LG*, 29 January 1799; 10 September 1799.

[48]*LGRT*, 18 April 1801.

[49]*LGRT*, 29 September 1800.

[50]*Columbian Museum and Savannah Advertiser*, 13 May 1803.

[51]*LG*, 1 June 1803.

[52]*LGRT*, 8 June 1803.

[53]*LGRT*, 27 April 1803.

[54]*LG*, 9 September 1800.

[55]*LGRT*, 24 December 1800.

[56]*SGLJ*, 10 December 1799.

[57]*LG*, 27 August 1799.

[58]*LG*, 3 September 1799; 17 September 1799; 27 August 1799; 25 February 1800.

[59]*LG*, 9 April 1799.

[60]*LGRT*, 28 October 1800.

[61]*LGRT*, 28 February 1800.

[62]*LGRT*, 9 June 1802.

[63]*LGRT*, 16 March 1803.

[64]*LGRT*, 23 March 1803.

[65]*LG*, 9 July 1799.

[66]Melish, *Travels*, 39-40.   [67]Ibid.

[68]Dr. D. G. Phillips, "The History of Bethel Associate Reformed Presbyterian Church." This is an original document written in the Bethel Church Register that was in use from 1853 until 1964.

[69]Kilpatrick, *Hephzibah*, 17.

[70]Ibid., 249.

[71]*House of Representatives Journal*, 11 February 1796, 102.

[72]*LG*, 16 April 1799.

[73]*LGRT*, 7 April 1802.

[74]*LG*, 16 April 1799, and 18 March 1800; *LGRT*, 5 November 1800, and 21 February 1801.

[75]*LGRT*, 12 November 1800

[76]*LG*, 15 August 1801.

[77]*LGRT*, 20 January 1802.

[78]*LGRT*, 2 May 1804.

[79]*LG*, 28 January 1800.

[80]*LGRT*, 15 June 1803.

[81]*LGRT*, 1 August 1804.

[82]Francis Asbury, *The Journal of Rev. Francis Asbury, Bishop of the Methodist Episcopal Church from August 7, 1771 to December 7, 1815* (New York, 1821) 2:67.

[83]Ibid, 3:126.

[84]Lorenzo Dow, *History of Cosmopolite; or the Four Volumes of Lorenzo's Journal Concentrated into One. From Childhood to 1814* (New York, 1814) 174.

[85]Ibid., 175.

[86]Watkins, *Digest*, 320.

[87]*House of Representatives Journal*, 5 February 1796, 85.

[88]Marchbury and Crawford, *Digest*, 560-62.

[89]*Executive Department Minutes*, 23 September 1796–13 October 1797, 143.

[90]E. Merton Coulter, "The Birth of a University," *Georgia Historical Quarterly* 46/2 (June 1962): 147.

[91]*House of Representatives Journal*, 15 February 1799, 78.

[92]*LG*, 3 December 1799.

[93]Coulter, "The Birth of a University," 146.

[94]*Georgia Gazette*, 3 July 1800.

[95]Coulter, "The Birth of a University," 147.

[96]*LGRT*, 27 June 1801.

[97]R. P. Brooks, "Abraham Baldwin, Statesman & Educator," *Georgia Historical Quarterly* 11/2 (1927): 178.

[98]*House of Representatives Journal*, 10 February 1796, 96.

[99]Marchbury and Crawford, *Digest*, 567-68; Watkins, *Digest*, 615.

[100]Charles Edgeworth Jones, *Education in Georgia* (Washington: Government Printing Office, 1889) 21-22.

[101]Knight, *Georgia's Landmarks*, 1:705.

[102]W. G. Boogher, *Secondary Education in Georgia, 1732–1858,* (Philadelphia, 1933) 49; E. Merton Coulter, "The Ante-Bellum Academy Movement in Georgia," *Georgia Historical Quarterly*, 5/4 (1921): 11-42.

[103]Knight, *Georgia's Landmarks*, 1:705; *Executive Department Minutes*, 16 March 1797, 161; 8 February 1798, 138.

[104]*LGRT*, 5 August 1800

[105]Watkins, *Digest*, 22 February 1796, 15; Boogher, *Secondary Education in Georgia,* 63-64.

[106]*House of Representatives Journal*, 11 February 1797, 355.

[107]Watkins, *Digest*, 615.

[108]Clayton, *Compilation*, 126, 127, 496.

[109]Watkins, *Digest*, 615.

[110]*News and Farmer* (Louisville GA), 27 October 1921.

[111]Smith Notebook in Louisville Library.

[112]*LGRT*, 27 May 1800.

[113]*LGRT*, 26 May 1802.

[114]*LGRT*, 22 August 1804.

[115]*Columbian Museum and Savannah Advertiser*, 6 August 1806 and 9 August 1806.

[116]*LG*, 29 January 1799.

[117]*LG*, 23 July 1799.

[118]*LG*, 10 December 1799.

[119]*LG*, December 1799.

[120]*LG*, 28 May 1799.

[121]*SGLJ*, 24 December 1799; *LGRT*, 7 March 1801.

[122]*LGRT*, 30 May 1801.   [123]Ibid.

[124]*LGRT*, 25 August 1802.

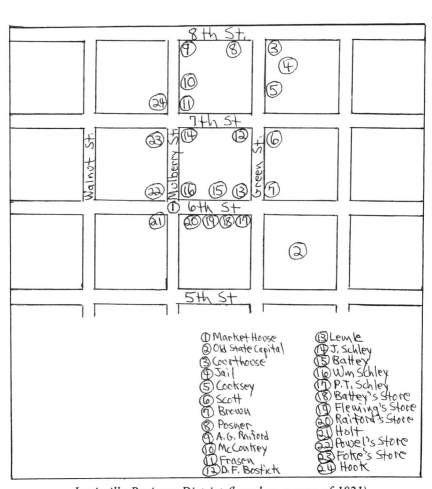

Louisville Business District (based on a map of 1821)

4
After the Departure of the Capital

Governmental Life

From the beginning, the selection of Louisville as Georgia's state capital was not a universally accepted decision, and opposition continued to be voiced even after the state house was completed and the governor and legislature moved to the new city. This was particularly true of the leadership in Savannah and Augusta, Georgia's two largest and most important towns. This dissatisfaction from leaders in the state's largest cities was combined with other factors disadvatangeous to Louisville. People increasingly believed that Louisville's location so close to Rocky Comfort Creek and the Ogeechee River made it rather unhealthy and that malaria symptoms were developing in the area. Others pointed out that the Louisville state house had not cost very much and had always been very unsatisfactory.[1] Which if any of these circumstances contributed directly to the decision to move the capital from Louisville to Milledgeville is uncertain, but it is believed that the main reason for the relocation was the fact that the tide of Georgia's population was moving rapidly toward the west and north, thus removing Louisville from the central and convenient location it had once enjoyed.[2]

With these ideas circulating among the legislators, proposals were made to move the capitol to various places. In 1802, an Augusta legislator presented an act "to move the seat of government from the town of Louisville to the city of Augusta."[3] His idea satisfied few people, and consequently the bill was defeated. The suggestion was then made that the capital be moved to some of the new land that had been acquired from the Indians.

As they began to look for a suitable site, the legislators just happened to commission the development of a new town, to be named Milledgeville in honor of current governor John Milledge. The act for this new town was passed on 11 May 1803, and it stated that five commissioners

> shall at the most eligible and suitable place, at or near the head of navigation on the south side of the Oconee River, lay out a tract of land, . . . which is hereby reserved and set apart for a town to be called and known by the name Milledgeville.[4]

This action took place just as the call for a new location for the capital was becoming very strong, so it seemed rather natural for this new city to be picked as a replacement for Louisville. On 12 December 1804, the Georgia legislature passed an act to make the town of Milledgeville "the permanent seat of government of this State."[5]

This change, just like the shift of the capital from Augusta to Louisville, was not to be very swift. Milledgeville was a new town and had few people or buildings. Plans for the state capital had to be drawn up, and the buildings had to be constructed. None of these things could be done quickly. In fact, it was not until 7 December 1805 that the legislature appropriated $15,000.00 for the erection of a new state house.[6] Thus, the move was delayed and the legislature was still meeting and passing laws in Louisville on 8 December 1806. As late as 3 April 1807, the Executive Department of Georgia was still meeting in Louisville.[7] The Georgia legislature met for the first time in the unfinished state house in Milledgeville in November of 1807.[8]

Even though it was no longer the bustling, cultured capital city for Georgia, Louisville continued to play an important role in the state. It really underwent a transition from being a community largely preoccupied with governmental matters at the state level to being a county-seat town that developed a successful agriculture-based economy dependent on the production of cotton. In this chapter we will consider the changes that took place in Louisville from 1807 to 1820 after the departure of the capital.

Continuing Work of Louisville Commissioners

As the capital moved away to Milledgeville, the commissioners of Louisville continued their work. Even though the tense political situation no longer existed in Louisville, there were at times some governmental and political problems in the town. This can clearly be seen in August of 1811, when people grew concerned about safety in their community and about the fact that the commissioners of Louisville were not doing their jobs very well. On 5 August 1811, an announcement was made that "the inhabitants of Louisville are requested to meet at the Market House on Friday next for the purpose of appointing commissioners of this town."[9] As a result of this town meeting, two slates of nominees were submitted to the governor of Georgia.

One group of citizens wrote to Governor David B. Mitchell on 9 August 1811, saying that of the five positions for commissioners of Louisville three were vacant because of the "resignation of Doctor John Powell, the removal of John Shelman, and the death of Chesley Bostwick." They wanted to see these vacancies filled so that "the powers vested in the said body may no longer be suspended." To fill these vacancies they recommended Ambrose Wright, Robert Fleming, and Archibald Campbell.[10]

In another letter to Governor Mitchell on 10 August 1811, other citizens expressed their interest in having a

> well organized town order consequent therefrom and conscious also that the same cannot be attained in this place but by a revival of that police, which did once exist, but which for years has laid dormant for the want of execution.

They believed that this situation could be corrected if L. B. Bostick, Thomas Hancock, and William Battey were appointed to fill the vacancies on the Louisville commissioners.[11]

Louisville faced the same problem on 8 February 1817, when a group of local citizens again wrote to Governor David B. Mitchell telling him that because of the

> death of Maj. John Berrien and the removal of Capt. David Clarke and Mr. Joseph White, the board of Commissioners of the said Town is incomplete, there being now only two Commissioners to wit, Col. Michael Shelman and Maj. Ambrose Wright.

They pointed out that this was not a "sufficient number to transact business." They also stated that it was very necessary that the board of commissioners be complete "to pass such ordinances for the government and regulation of the said town as may be right and salutary." To fill these vacancies, they recommended to the governor the names of Thomas Hancock, William N. Harman, and Major Wm. Schley. After the nominations were made to Governor Mitchell, he left office without taking action, so a citizen group proposed the same names to acting Governor Rabun, and he appointed them to fill the vacancies.[12]

The "Minutes" of the Louisville commissioners of 1 April 1817 indicates that this new board then began to take some action. They were concerned about regulating the town of Louisville, and to do this they appointed a committee to draw up ordinances:

> To prevent the pernicious and dangerous practice of running Horses and Horse racing within the limits of the Town of Louisville—an ordinance levying a tax on peddlers and showmen—an ordinance to prohibit the indecent practice of letting stud Horses to mares in the public view—an ordinance to prevent persons from discharging fire arms within the Limits of Said Town, and also an ordinance fixing the fees of the Marshall.

On 4 April 1817, the commissioners drafted an "ordinance to prevent the improper practice of trading on the Sabbath day," and on 3 December 1818, they passed an ordinance "to prevent dogs from being at large in the town of Louisville."[13] These ordinances clearly indicate that although the capital had moved, much of the rowdiness and other problems had remained in Louisville.

The Louisville commissioners, on 28 June 1820, were concerned about making some repairs to the market house. They put out to the "lowest bidder" the following specifications:

> Shingled with heart pine shingles the cupola newly weatherboarded, and Venetian blinds put to the windows, the house to be weather boarded from the bottom as high up as the old benches, new benches to be put all round 20 inches wide, made of two inch plank, a door to be made and hung to the place where the old door is, if any of the rafters or other timbers are rotten new ones are to be put in their place.[14]

It is clear from these specifications that many changes have been made in the market house since 1820.

Another example of some of the problems Louisville experienced came when it was discovered that some of the earliest records of the land on which the town of Louisville was located, which had originally been granted to David Russell, could not be found. This meant that no property owner in Louisville could prove evidence of title to his/her land. To correct this situation, an act was passed on 8 December 1815 to the effect that

> in all actions for the recovery of lots of land in the said town of Louisville, the parties to the action shall not be required to go further

back, in deducing title, than to the title from Roger Lawson and wife to the commissioners of the said town.[15]

Lawson had bought this land after it had been confiscated from Russell because of his Tory sympathies.

State House and Courthouse

The capital having been removed from Louisville, the Georgia government was now faced with the problem of deciding what to do with the old state house and other state property in Louisville. On 10 December 1807, the legislature passed an act "to dispose" of the state house and public square in the town of Louisville. The act stated that since the seat of the government had been removed to Milledgeville, "the late State House in the town of Louisville has become useless." Because of this, the old state house was to be "set apart as a public arsenal and place of deposit for all military stores belonging to the State of Georgia."[16]

Jefferson County and Louisville still had no courthouse nor a good place to hold courts and elections. In 1808 the inferior court ordered that courts and elections would be held at the Louisville Academy. In 1809, court sessions were transferred to the "Old Coffee House," then occupied by William Wilkie. The residence of Daniel Lemle was next used for a brief period, and then the courts were again held at the "Old Coffee House," occupied at that time by William Schley. From 1813–1816, the county used the old state house as a place for courts and elections. The state authorized the sale of the old state house in 1813, and it was bought by the St. Patrick Masonic Lodge No. 2.[17]

As early as 1800, the Inferior Court of Jefferson County ordered $300 to be paid to a committee for erecting a courthouse, but not until 1816 was the first courthouse of the county built. On 20 February of that year—exactly twenty years after the creation of the county—the inferior court accepted the structure from the contractor, Isaac Rawls, Jr. This building was used until the fall of 1824, when the county again began to use the old state house. A contract was made in November 1824, providing for the purchase of the old state house for $1,500, the Masonic Lodge retaining the use of a room on the upper floor. The original courthouse building was ordered sold for $100 to a group for use as a church, but eight years later this order was revoked on the grounds that the terms of the contract had not been fulfilled, and the building was resold to Johathan Robertson for the same amount.[18]

Taxes in Louisville and Jefferson County

One would think that the movement of the capital away from Louisville would adversely affect the economy and population in both Louisville and Jefferson County. The population continued to increase, but the local economy was clearly hurt by this action.

Many changes took place between 1804 and 1809, and the tax digests point these out. In 1809, there were 834 households in Jefferson County as compared with 799 in 1804, a 4% increase. Of these households, 264 (or 32%) owned land outside the county, while only 95 (or 12%) were in this position in 1804. It is very difficult to explain this 180% increase in land ownership outside the county unless some of the people decided it was in their financial interest to acquire land in the newly developing western lands. In 1809, 326 slave owners (or 39% of the households) possessed approximately 1,859 slaves. This compares with 296 slave owners (or 37% of the households) owning 1,708 slaves in 1804. Even with these increases, the taxes collected in the county were $1,615.59 or only $22.31 more than in 1804. Thus, although the households and number of slaves increased, very little additional tax revenue was collected. This unstable economic situation is further shown by the fact that many houses and lots in Louisville changed hands and by the fact that most of the old shop owners were gone and new ones had appeared.[19]

The *Jefferson County Tax Digest* of 1814 also showed many changes taking place. The county was increasing in population, but the local economy was experiencing some real problems. There were now 982 householders in Jefferson County, which was 148 more than in 1809 (or an 18% increase). Of these, only 185 owned land outside the county. This number was 79 less than in 1809. There were 375 households (or 38%) that owned slaves, and this was 49 more than in 1809. The slave population of the county was now 2,420, which was 561 more than in 1809. Thus, the period from 1809 to 1814 showed an increase in households in Jefferson County, a decrease in those who owned land outside the county, an increase in slave owners, and a large increase in the number of slaves in the county.[20]

One would think that the above figures should point to a big boost in the economy, but such is not the case. The total tax digest for 1814 was $1,670.02, only $54.43 more than in 1809. This is only a 3% increase. While the households increased by 18% and the slave population increased by 30%, the taxes increased by only 3%. One should immediately ask why. One key reason is that 55 (or 6%) of the landowners were listed as defaulters on their taxes. In addition, whereas there were 13 stores with $22,975 worth of stock in 1809, there were only 11 stores with $11,400 worth of stock in 1814. Only four of the store owners who were operating in 1814 had been open in 1809. Thus the economy was not in good shape.[21]

Many more changes took place between 1814 and 1820 in the economics of Louisville and Jefferson County, as the tax digests of these years clearly show. There were 1,265 households in Jefferson County in 1820, which was 283 more than in 1814 (or a 22% increase). Of these households 445 had no land. There were 122 who owned land outside the county, compared with 185 in 1814. Slave owners numbered 414 (or 33%) as compared with 375 (or 38%) in 1814. The slave population also increased to 2,682, which was 262 more than in 1814. The period from 1814 to 1820 showed an increase of households in the county, a decrease in those who owned land outside the county, and an increase in the number of slave owners and in the number of slaves in the county.[22]

The total tax for the county was $1,973.26, which was $303.24 more than the tax in 1814.[23] This was also the highest amount of taxes that had ever been paid in Jefferson County. All of this information clearly shows the positive economic impact that the cotton economy was having on this thriving agricultural community.

Business Activity

When the capital moved from Louisville in 1807, the prosperous economy of the town changed dramatically. The tax digest of 1809 points out that there were then only four general merchandise stores in Louisville. James Meriwether was the only merchant who had weathered the bad economic storm, and the value of his stock was $1,000 less than it had been in 1804. All of the other merchants were new, and they owned only small quantities of merchandise.

The people of Louisville, however, could have hope for a better future, because new businesses began coming to their town. In 1801, David M'Cormick notified Louisville that he was opening a store at the corner of Seventh and Mulberry.[24] That same year James B. McCreedy "tailor and ladies habit-maker" informed Louisville that he had "taken the shop next door above Mr. Olmstead's Tavern and that he is in need of a journeyman." Roger Olmstead also announced that he had taken over the "well known house" of Joseph G. Posner and that he planned to keep a "house of entertainment for planters, merchants, and others of a genteel cast." He also said that he would take good care of their horses and provide "choice liquors."[25] By 1810 William N. Harman began his general merchandise store in Louisville.[26]

In 1811, one Thomas M'Murrey informed the community that his health had been restored, and he had moved "to a commodious shop, in the Coffee House, next door to the Court Room, and opposite the State House Square, he intends to be more punctual in future in carrying on the Clocks and Watch Making, together with the Silver Smith and Jewelry Business." The "tailor and habit maker" Jacob M'Collough also informed the public that he was continuing to do business "at this old stand on Red Row."[27]

By 1814 Louisville's economic fortunes were improving. There were now five general merchandise stores. One should note, however, that all of the merchants were different from those in 1809 and that most of their stocks of merchandise were small. Louisville had gone through some very rough economic times, but it was beginning to build on a new business base.

Apparently those new businessmen inspired optimism in the whole community, as can be seen from an article in a Louisville newspaper of May 1816:

> With a view to give a clear idea of our town abroad, we think it necessary, since the usual criteria of judging its importance is derived, to state that there are now in Louisville ten considerable stores of dry goods and groceries—a manufactory of cottons—one of hats--one of shoes and boots. Add to these furniture and carriages are made here, painting, house carpentering and blacksmithing are executed in all their barron [sic] branches, together with other branches of business important in a well regulated community.

The writer also pointed out that "there are no empty houses in Louisville, and building is going on."[28]

In 1816, Etheldred Moore and Hugh Murphy had an "establishment for boots and shoes" at the "Old State House."[29] Earlier in the year C. W. McMurrain had opened up a "boot & shoe business."[30] In the same year

Jacob McCollough announced he was setting up as a "tailor opposite Old Printing Office, near the Court House," and McDaniel and Henson set up as "Tailors & Habit Makers at the Public House of John P. Harvey."[31] James B. Hall also announced that he had purchased the tan-yard of Abram Robinson and that he planned to continue a "tanning and currying business" there.[32]

Especially as the capital moved away, the leaders of Louisville looked for a way to keep the town prosperous, and they were certain that port facilities would do it. Thus the leaders of Louisville formed "The Ogeechee Navigation Company." In February 1811 there was a meeting of the commissioners of the Ogeechee Navigation company, held at "Mr. Posner's Long Room" in the town of Louisville. Those present were Walter Robinson, John Berrien, John Powell, Little B. Bostick Sr., and Michael Shelman. It was their desire to get passed an act "to incorporate a company for the purpose of opening the Ogeechee River, from the mouth of Canouchee to the mouth of Rocky Comfort, and for the improvement of the navigation thereof."[33]

The Ogeechee Navigation Company continued to work at least through 1816 and did actually start clearing the Ogeechee River. The Louisville newspaper of that time gave the following notice: "Ogeechee Navigation Co.—The share-holders notifies that an election for new board of directors will be held at the house of John P. Harvey in Louisville."[34] In the July 1816 edition of this Louisville paper, John G. Bostick, agent for clearing out the Ogeechee River, advertized for "10 able-bodied Negro men for $14.00 per month will be given and also liberal pieces will be given for Bacon & Whiskey."[35]

This work on the river gave the people of Louisville renewed hope about their future and encouraged them, as can be seen in an 1816 edition of the *American Advocate*:

> With regard to the Ogeechee River, we confidently hope that it will yet be made the answer to navigation. Should this great object be carried into effect, Louisville will yet become a place of immense depot and of course, great trade. Some boats, heavy laden with cotton, slaves, etc. have already descended this river, without accident, and with little or no interruption.[36]

Even as late as 1829, there was still an emphasis on Ogeechee navigation. Adiel Sherwood's *Gazetteer of the State of Georgia* of that year said, "Ten thousand dollars were raised by subscribers, to clear the

Ogechee of obstructions, and boats have descended from Louisville to Savannah with 200 and 300 bags cotton."[37]

The river may have eventually been cleaned and boats may have come to Louisville, but there were never many of them and the bonanza that the town hoped for never came. Slowly the people dropped their hope for a port altogether.

In 1793, something happened that would have a much greater impact on Jefferson County and Louisville than navigation on the Ogeechee River—the invention of the cotton gin. Prior to this time little cotton was grown in Georgia because of the difficulty of separating the lint from the seed, even though it was known that Georgia's soil and climate were well suited for cotton. But with the coming of the cotton gin, all this changed.

By 1820, the economy of Louisville had picked up a great deal, probably because of the success with cotton-growing in Jefferson County. This seems to have brought in a great deal of money to the county and to Louisville, with the result that many stores were operating in the town. Although the tax digest does not spell out exactly what types of stores were operating in Louisville, it does identify some twenty-two different stores that had "trade" or stock with a total tax evaluation of $46,150, which was by far the largest store stocks that Louisville had ever had. It appears that although the departure of the capital took away the importance and prestige of Louisville and almost destroyed its economy, cotton farming returned Louisville to prosperity and made it into a successful small agricultural town. Its prosperous economy had returned, but those glorious days were gone forever.

Cotton clearly gave a major boost to the economy of the area, and, as this happened, the site of Old Town began to have some activity and importance again. After having been George Galphin's key site for trade and diplomacy, Old Town had lost most of its importance after the Revolutionary War. It was willed to John Galphin, but he lost interest in it and moved to some large landholding that he and his brother were given in Washington County. As a result, he ran into some financial problems and was forced to sell Old Town in 1786.

This property was then bought by Robert Forsyth of Augusta as an investment. He acted as an absentee landlord and did little to maintain his newly purchased land as he pursued his business interests in Augusta.[38]

His son John later built a plantation house and other buildings at Old Town, but he and his family lived there for only a few years. When he ran into financial problems, he decided to sell Old Town rather than risk his promising political career.[39]

The new owner of Old Town was Christopher Fitzsimons of Charleston, who paid $1,700 for this land and started a new era in this plantation's history.[40] His family actually owned Old Town for three generations. Although Old Town had been basically unmanaged for twenty years, most of Jefferson County had developed into a flourishing agricultural community.

Fitzsimons followed the example of the rest of the county and transformed this plantation from semiwild acreage into a dynamic cotton producing area. He was able to accomplish that, the tax digest of 1814 reveals, because he had 89 slaves who cleared and planted cotton and other crops on his 3,126 acres.[41] In 1810, Fitzsimons discovered a "burhstone" outcropping on his property. He began quarrying these stones as millstones after some experts from Philadelphia said that they were superior in quality to the millstones that were imported from France. This discovery heightened the interest of Louisville leaders in making the Ogeechee River navigable for larger ships.[42] Apparently the quarrying operation was short-lived, but the Fitzsimon family kept their interest in Old Town for a long time.[43]

Printing and Newspapers

Newspapers continued to work and print their editions even though Louisville was no longer the capital nor had its former importance. These newspapers continued to struggle financially, and they were continually changing names and owners. In 1810, Ambrose Day changed the name of the newspaper from the *Louisville Gazette and Republican Trumpet* back to the original name the *Louisville Gazette*. His newspaper continued to advertise the "collector's" and "sheriff's" sales that took place at the market house, and his office remained as the bookstore of Louisville and Jefferson County.[44]

A new newspaper called the *Louisville Courier* began on 21 August 1811. It was published by George W. Wheeler for Harvey and Dowsing. The editor made it known that his paper would include domestic and foreign news and political pieces that would be "carefully selected, that none may appear which will be calculated to rob the paper of its impartial Republican character," as well as religious, political, and literary essays and poetical writing. The editor noted that he already had 100 subscribers, but that he was planning to print 200 copies of the paper in hopes that none would be left.[45] It should be mentioned that the existing issues of this paper are full of legal notices and foreign news along with a few literary pieces. They contain virtually no local news and only a few advertisements.

Apparently the *Louisville Gazette* was sold by Ambrose Day to the group Mr. Wheeler represented. The *Louisville Gazette* ceased publication about the same time the *Louisville Courier* began. Additionally, Ambrose Day advertized in the *Louisville Courier* that he was beginning a new newspaper in Eatonton, Georgia, and that people could buy subscriptions to it at the office of the *Louisville Courier*.[46] No information exists about the *Louisville Courier* in 1812, but a new paper called the *American Standard* began publication that year under the editorship of A. Wright and D. Clarke. In 1816, the *American Advocate* appeared with George W. Wheeler and James Clarke serving as editors.

Turnover in editors appears to have been high, and many changes in names occurred in the Louisville newspapers of this period. The papers also were continuingly struggling to survive financially. Apparently, the newspaper business in Louisville experienced much instability as "those glorious days" ended for this community.

Louisville's Professionals

Because of the laxity of material about the period from 1807 until 1820, not too much is known concerning the professional people that lived in Louisville during this time. The available information indicates only a small number of lawyers in Louisville during this period, particularly once the capital moved to Milledgeville. The *Louisville Gazette* of December 1810 stated that J. Child had recently opened a law office in Louisville.[47] John Shly announced that "he is admitted to the practice of Law, and will give the most unremitted attention to any business that may be put in his hand." He also informed the public that he was a "man of moderate talents, and that his fees will be moderate in proportion to his talents."[48] A Louisville newspaper in 1812 stated that William Schley had been admitted to law and was now practicing in Louisville.[49] What happened to these lawyers is not clear, but the only one listed in the tax digest of 1814 was William Schley.[50] Mr. Schley was also listed in the 1820 tax digest as a lawyer in Louisville, along with two newcomers, A. L. Gamble and William H. Jackson.[51]

Doctors were more numerous but only slightly so. In 1809, there were five doctors in Louisville: John Pugsley, Micaiah H. Powell, Josiah M. Sterrett, Eli M. Carcibzea, and John Powell.[52] A Dr. B. D. Thompson came to Louisville in 1810.[53] In the 1814 tax digest, John Powell, Josiah M. Sterrett, B. D. Thompson, and John Pugsley were listed as Louisville doctors.[54] By 1820, the number and names of doctors had changed. John Pugsley and B. D. Thompson were the only doctors remaining from the 1814 list, but new doctors included Robert Lowery, Lloyd Belt, John Jenkins, Daniel Hook, and Louis Kennon.[55]

Religious Life

As has already been mentioned, there was no church in Louisville until 1811. Before that time, people worshiped at the state house or at churches in the rural areas around Louisville. Many people were dissatisfied with this arrangement, and finally some of the leading citizens got together early in 1810 and decided that their city must have a house of public worship. They drew up a document in which people agreed to pay a certain amount of money to aid in the building of a church. They set up a committee composed of James Meriwether, John Powell, and Philip Scott to be in charge of the undertaking.[56]

An interesting point about this church was that it was to be a community place of worship open to all denominations rather than just one. It was clearly stated by the group

> that every denomination of churches who have the privilege of preaching in the meeting house in the town of Louisville are also at liberty to hold their private meetings in said house with closed doors, or otherwise, without molestation or hinderance, provided they do not interfere with public worship.[57]

To make this building possible many people in the community gave from two to fifty dollars. The largest contributors were John Berrien, John Powell, Philip Scott, James Jackson, James Meriwether, Walter Robinson, William N. Harman, and Ambrose Day. Even the Jewish merchant J. G. Posner gave fifteen dollars for this place of worship.

At a meeting on 19 February 1810, the committee came to agreement on the plans of the church and the materials to be used in it. It was to be 50 feet long and 35 feet wide, and the pitch was to be 20 feet. It was to have twelve large windows and six small ones and three folding doors.

They decided to put an advertisement in the *Louisville Gazette* requesting people willing to contract for the church to give their bids by 1 March 1810. They also specified the materials to go into the church as follows: "the sills and shingles to be of good sound cypress, the other lumber to be prime yellow pine."[58]

This committee met again on 4 May 1810 and decided that the house of public worship should be 40 feet in length and 30 in width and that this plan would be available with the secretary of the board, Mr. Day, "for the purpose of receiving proposals for building the same, the former plan having been considered too large."[59]

At a meeting on 4 June 1810, the committee decided to put the church on the campus of Louisville Academy, about two hundred feet east of where the old brick academy building stood and facing Cherry Street.

The committee had received several proposals for building the church, but that of Captain John A. Cobb was the lowest at $650, so the committee decided to give him the contract for building Louisville's first place of worship. The committee agreed to pay Mr. Cobb $100 to start the church, $200 "on the raising of the house," and $350 within one month after the completion of the church, for a total of $650.[60]

Apparently Captain Cobb began to work soon after the signing of the contract and built a very acceptable structure. On 11 December 1810, the building committee announced that the church had been completed according to the specifications of the contract, and that they had agreed to accept the building and pay Captain Cobb his money.

At last, Louisville had a church, but there were no furnishings in it. On the same day that the committee accepted the church building from the contractor, another committee composed of James Meriweather and Walter Robinson was appointed to contract for "erecting a pulpit and making sufficient number of benches for the house of public worship."[61]

On 6 May 1811, this committee contracted with John Schley to build the pews. He was to make two types of pews. The side pews were to have doors on them and were to cost six dollars each. The center pews were without doors and were five dollars each. The decision was made on 13 June 1811 that seven of the center pews would be used as public pews open for anyone in the community but that the remaining pews, would be advertised for sale on the following terms: "one-third cash, one-third at 60 days, and one-third at One Hundred and Twenty Days."[62]

On 29 June 1811, the sale was held in the new church building and the 21 pews were sold to the highest bidders. The price per pew ran from ten to seventeen dollars. The total amount earned from the sale of the pews were $306.25.

After the sale of the pews, some people in the community were very unhappy because they had not had the opportunity to purchase one of the pews. Therefore the church committee decided that five of the pews intended for public use should be sold to those desiring them. By the fall of 1811, the pews were finished and services could finally be held in Louisville's first church.

Even after Louisville ceased to be the capital, itinerant preachers continued to pass through and preached at the community church. It was announced that Rev. Mr. Storrs would preach in Louisville on Thursday, 14 March 1811, and on the Sunday following at the Presbyterian meeting house called Bethel.[63] The Methodist Bishop Francis Asbury and the Rev. Mr. Myers spoke at the church in Louisville on 21 November 1811, and the Rev. Mr. Russel was to speak there on the next Tuesday and Wednesday.[64] As Asbury made his last trip to Georgia, he visited Louisville on 30 November 1814, but he was very disappointed by the small crowd and few converts that he had there.[65] The newspaper noted that Rev. Thomas Darley would preach at "the Church in this place." This same issue announced "a Methodist Camp Meeting at Providence Meeting House in the Fork of Rocky-Comfort and Ogeechee" about four miles from Louisville.[66] Rev. Messrs. Roberts and Roberts were to preach at the Church in Louisville in July of 1816.[67] The Rev. Mr. Beaman of the Presbyterian Church was to preach in Louisville in April of 1816.[68]

In 1817, Ways Baptist Church was constituted. This church, a structure of logs, was used for school and religious purposes. For a number of years prior to its organization, services had been held regularly at what was known then as Darcy's Meeting House. The majority of the original members had come from Brushy Creek Church in Burke County. There were forty-six members, thirteen males and thirty-three females.[69]

It should be noted that there was a Masonic lodge in Louisville from at least as early as 1814. It was St. Patrick's Lodge No. 8, and records were filed on it from 1814 through 1820. In 1821 the number of the lodge was changed to No. 2, and it had about thirty members.[70]

With the relocation of the capital from Louisville, the official publications of the state ceased having much information about Louisville. Additionally, newspapers in other towns lost interest in Louisville.

Although newspapers continued to be printed in Louisville, few of these survived between 1807 and 1820. Thus, there is a general dearth of material about this period making it impossible to write very much about the governmental and daily life of Louisville during this time. Many things lost their importance in this community, such as the militias, and other things received much less attention, such as entertainment and education. This laxity of information clearly indicates that although Louisville and Jefferson County had been rejuvenated economically, "those glorious days" that the town had experienced politically, culturally, and educationally were gone forever. Even though Louisville would not be forgotten, it would never again have the fame that it experienced as Georgia's capital.

Notes

[1]Smith, *The Story of Georgia*, 234.

[2]Knight, *Georgia Landmarks*, 157.

[3]*House of Representatives Journal* 4 November 1802, 10, and 10 November 1802, 23.

[4]Clayton, *Compilation*, 107.

[5]Clayton, *Compilation*, 209.

[6]Leela S. Beeson, "The Old State Capitol in Milledgeville and Its Cost," *Georgia Historical Quarterly* 34/3 (1950): 195-96.

[7]*LGRT*, 22 May 1807.

[8]Beeson, "The Old State Capital," 196.

[9]MSS in File 11 in the Georgia Department of Archives.

[10]Ibid.   [11]Ibid.   [12]Ibid.

[13]*Minutes of the Louisville Commissioners.*   [14]Ibid.

[15]Lucius Q. C. Lamar, *A Compilation of the Laws of the State of Georgia 1810 through 1819, Inclusive* (Augusta, 1821).

[16]*Columbian Museum and Savannah Advertiser*, 15 December 1807.

[17]Ibid., 5 (1807–1810) 22 and 54; 6 (1810–1813) 77, 83; Lamar, *A Compilation*, 971.

[18]*Inferior Court Minutes*, 1 (1790–1800) 174; 7 (1814–1818) 53-54; 9 (1820–1835) 157-58 and 179; 10, (1835–1840) 21.

[19]*Jefferson County Tax Digest* of 1804 and 1809.

[20]*Jefferson County Tax Digests* of 1809 and 1814.   [21]Ibid.

[22]*Jefferson County Tax Digests* of 1814 and 1820.   [23]Ibid.

[24]*LG*, 22 May 1807.   [25]*LGRT*, 15 May 1807.

[26]*LG*, 20 December 1810.   [27]*LC*, 25 September 1811.

[28]*American Advocate* (Louisville GA) 9 May 1816. Hereafter *American Advocate* will be abbreviated as *AA*.

[29]*AA*, 21 November 1816. [30]*AA*, 29 February 1816.

[31]*AA*, 22 February 1816. [32]*AA*, 21 March 1816.

[33]*LG*, 2 February 1811. [34]*AA*, 25 April 1816.

[35]*AA*, 4 July 1816. [36]*AA*, 9 May 1816.

[37]Adiel Sherwood, *Gazetteer of the State of Georgia* (1829, Reprinted in Athens in 1939) 85.

[38]*Augusta Chronicle and Gazette of the State*, 25 July 1807; *LGRT*, 15 May 1807.

[39]*Jefferson County Superior Court Records* (1803–1809), 332-35.

[40]Christopher Fitzsimons Letterbooks (1799–1813), in the South Carolinians Library, Columbia.

[41]*Jefferson County Tax Digest* of 1814.

[42]Christopher Fitzsimons Letterbooks and *Republican and Savannah Evening Ledger*, 29 June 1811.

[43]John McKay Sheftall, "Ogeechee Old Town: A Georgia Plantation," a paper delivered at the Georgia Historical Society Meeting in October 1981 in Louisville.

[44]*LG*, 4 May 1810. [45]*Louisville Courier*, 21 August 1811.

[46]*LC*, 9 October 1811. [47]*LG*, 11 December 1810.

[48]*Louisville Courier*, 23 October 1811.

[49]*American Standard*, 14 May 1812.

[50]*Jefferson County Tax Digest*, 1814.

[51]*Jefferson County Tax Digest*, 1820.

[52]*Jefferson County Tax Digest*, 1809.

[53]*LG*, 11 December 1810. [54]*Jefferson County Tax Digest*, 1814.

[55]*Jefferson County Tax Digest*, 1820.

[56]R.A. Rhodes, "Louisville's First Church," *News and Farmer*, 16 October 1930.

[57]*Minute Book*, 15 February 1810, *News and Farmer*, 16 October 1930.

[58]*Minute Book*, 19 February 1810.

[59]*LG*, 4 May 1810.

[60]*Minute Book*, 4 June 1810; see also MSS by Emily C. Farmer on "Early Religious Life of Jefferson County," July 1961, in Jefferson County Library.

[61]*Minute Book*, 11 December 1810.

[62]*Minute Book*, 13 June 1811.

[63]*LG*, 19 February 1811. [64]*LC*, 23 October 1811.

[65]Asbury *The Journal*, 3:371-72.

[66]*AA*, 20 June 1816. [67]*AA*, 18 July 1816. [68]Ibid.

[69]Kilpatrick, *Hephzibah*, 249.

[70]Papers of Mrs. Phillips Seebach in Louisville Library.

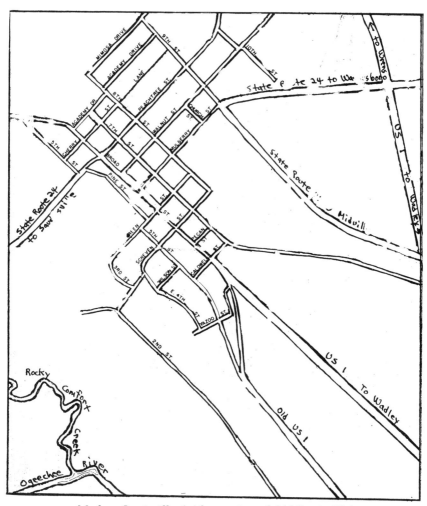

Modern Louisville (with remains of Old Louisville)

Appendix I
Interesting People
of Early Louisville and Jefferson County

During the early history of Louisville and Jefferson County, many interesting people played important roles in the activities of the area. Three of these people were Rev. David Bothwell, Gen. Solomon Wood, and Mr. Joseph G. Posner. Their lives and relationship with Louisville and Jefferson County will briefly be discussed in this appendix.

Reverend David Bothwell

In the religious history of early Louisville, one name always stands out: Rev. David E. Bothwell. Although he lived for only eleven years in the Louisville area, he became an influential citizen and was highly respected by the people there.

Born about 1750 in the county of Monaghan in Ireland, David Bothwell had a rather hard life. His father, who seems to have been a tenant of a small estate, died and left behind a widow and ten children. This meant that David had to go to work at an early age. With rigorous economy and hard work, he prepared himself to go into the ministry. Bothwell attended the University of Edinburgh and probably graduated with honors from there about 1786. He was then received as a student of theology by the presbytery of Monaghan and was licensed as minister in 1787.[1]

In 1788 the minister for the Presbyterian churches in what is now Jefferson and Burke counties moved, leaving the churches without a preacher. These churches then petitioned the presbyters of Monaghan for a minister, and David Bothwell was chosen to fill the place.

Reportedly, just before his appointment, Mr. Bothwell had become engaged to Jane Wright and worried that his new position might alter all their plans. Miss Wright agreed to accompany Mr. Bothwell to America, however, and the wedding was solemized in October 1789.[2] Soon after the wedding they set sail for their new home in Queensboro. They arrived in Charleston, South Carolina, on 25 December 1789 and shortly thereafter came to Queensborough to begin their new life.[3]

David Bothwell was apparently the minister of several Presbyterian churches in the Jefferson County area: Buckhead Creek, which had moved several times and finally located where Bethel Church now stands; Fleeting's Meeting House, which became Big Creek and later changed to Ebenezer; and Queensborough.[4] He also preached at many other places in Jefferson and Burke counties, including the state house in Louisville.[5]

Not only did Bothwell serve the Louisville area as a minister, but he also was an influential citizen. During the Yazoo scandal, Rev. Bothwell was requested to address the house of representatives of Georgia about "spiritual wickedness in high places." He is said to have used Proverbs 29:2 as his text: "When the righteous are in authority, the people rejoice, but when the wicked beareth rule, the people mourn." He delivered this sermon in the old state house just twenty-two days before the Yazoo Fraud Papers were burned on 11 February 1796. Mrs. Louisa M. Wright of Louisville, who was a distant relative of Rev. Bothwell, wrote that she had a copy of this sermon and that on the first page it stated that the sermon was by "Rev. David Bothwell, D. D., Pastor of the United Presbyterian Congregations of Buckhead and Louisville, Georgia." According to Mrs. Wright, the substance of the sermon, which was preached before the Georgia house of representatives in Louisville on 19 January 1796, was then published at the request of the hearers.[6]

David Bothwell was also appointed as a commissioner of Louisville Academy.[7] He was a highly educated man and was greatly respected as a teacher. In a letter written by Governor James Jackson to John Milledge on 13 March 1799 reference is made to Rev. Bothwell:

> I should have written you two days since by Dr. Bothwell, the minister of this place. . . . I beg you to show him what attention may be in your power as one of the Trustees of Huntington College. He has had my boys under him since the period of their coming up, and is a complete Latin Greek and Hebrew scholar, besides a knowledge of French—His character is very respectable though a plain Man—He has an invitation to Savannah and as his health is by no means stable here—he wishes to change the Air. I have been thinking that if he succeeds he might preach on Sunday & keep school at the orphan house where he might reside during the Week.[8]

His friend Rev. James Rodgers of White Hall Fairfield County in South Carolina had also expressed concern about Bothwell's health in an earlier letter. He wrote to Bothwell at his Queensborough address on 2

January 1792: "I am much surprised that you remain in Georgia when you enjoy such a poor state of health."[9]

The bad health continued for Rev. David Bothwell, and he died on 30 June 1801 at age forty-five while visiting in the home of his friend Governor Jared Irwin.[10] He was buried in the Irwin family cemetery in Washington County.[11] He left behind his pregnant wife, Jane, and four sons (Ebenezer, John Wright, James, and David Emanuel) and an unborn son Samuel. The newspaper noted that all who were indebted to David Bothwell should pay Jane Bothwell, Samuel Bothwell, or John Patterson.[12]

The will of David Bothwell was made on 30 June 1801 and probated on 2 November 1801. It was apparently made at the home of Gov. Jared Irwin in Washington County. In the will Jane Bothwell; John Patterson, Jr.; and Samuel Bothwell were named as executors. Samuel Robinson, William C. Kennedy, Jared Irwin, and William Irwin were witnesses to the will. In the will he gave to Jane Bothwell, his wife, the place on which she lived and all the profits from it. She was asked "to educate the children as much as lies in her power." If she should remarry, she was to receive "a Negro wench named Cate, a young bay mare, and two cows and calves to be at her disposal." The son Ebenezer was to receive 150 acres of land on the Ogeechee River joining Lawson and a Negro girl named Nane along with a tract of land "lying near the Eight Mile branch adjoing Clarke and Bryan." To his son John Wright he left the other half of the tract lying on the Ogeechee River and the other half of the tract on Eight Mile Branch, along with a Negro girl named Dinah. To the son James he bequeathed one half of the tract of land whereon the mother lived at his mother's death or remarriage, together with a Negro boy named George. Son David was to receive the other half of his mother's tract and a Negro named Jack. Bothwell noted in his will that his wife is pregnant and "should she be delivered and the child survive me it should have a Negro wench named Penny and a boy named Isaac."[13]

Jane Bothwell later married Rev. John Renwick and by him had additional children. She died on 12 December 1849.[14]

Reverend Bothwell's death was an untimely one, and his period of service was comparativelly short, but he left a definite imprint upon the affairs of both church and state in and around Louisville during those glorious days.

General Solomon Wood

Solomon Wood was born on 6 April 1756 in Virginia. His family later moved to North Carolina. At age sixteen he began serving in the North Carolina Infantry and soon became First Lieutenant.[15] During the Revolutionary War he distinquished himself as a soldier and rapidly rose through the ranks. By the end of the war, he had become captain.[16]

Why Solomon Wood moved to Jefferson County and established himself in Williamson Swamp about six miles from Galphin's Old Town is not clear. Neither is the exact date of his arrival in the area known, but he wrote a letter to the Georgia governor from his Jefferson County home in 1788. Very few original letters have survived from this early period of Jefferson County history, but the Georgia Department of Archives in Atlanta does possess one letter written by Solomon Wood on 14 March 1788 from "Woods fort on Williamson Swamp, Six miles from the Old Town." The letter, which was sent to the governor of Georgia in Augusta, deals with Indian trouble in Jefferson County. The letter tells about a Mr. Sikes and his family who were attacked by a party of Indians who came close to Wood's Fort. When one Allen Surlock tried to help the Sikes family, he, a young woman, and a little girl were shot and scalped. As a result of these incidents, Gen. Wood wrote the governor:

> In a defenceless Situation neighter [*sic*] assistance of men or ammunition and without which we can not atempt to tend the Little land we have opened to remove to a Distance from the Savages we can not having maney [*sic*] of Us Spent our all in geting [*sic*] hear [*sic*] if we are to cover the Settlements less exposed it is but reasonable we should be Supported by them—We have no Dought [*sic*] but Yr Honor & the Councle [*sic*] will give the necessary orders and we hope the Commanding officer may be obliged to have them Executed.[17]

Tradition has it that he built his home in Williamson Swamp on a high knoll a mile east of Bartow. It was a blockhouse built like a fort for the protection of the people from Indian raids, and it had a bell that could be heard about two miles. When signs of Indian trouble were seen or heard the bell would peal out its warning, and the people would seek safety in Wood's fort.[18]

The executive council of Georgia on 20 September 1790, granted 872 acres in Washington County to Solomon Wood.[19] In 1799 the Jefferson County tax digest listed Solomon Wood as living in Captain Raiford's

83rd Military district. The tax digest also indicates that Wood had the distinguished position of paying more taxes than anyone else in the district. He had to pay $12.15 taxes because he owned twenty slaves and 1,550 acres of land.[20]

By 1814 his possessions had increased to such an extent that he had to pay $127.51 tax. These taxes were paid on forty-seven slaves, 1,337 1/2 acres of third class land and 6,188 acres of pine land in Jefferson County, 500 acres of pine land in Tattnall County, 330 acres of pine land in Montgomery County, 405 acres of third class and 232 1/2 acres of pine land in Laurens County, 202 1/2 acres of third class land in Jasper County, and 202 1/2 acres of third class land in Twiggs County.[21]

Solomon Wood's distinquished military career and wealth enabled him to become one of the most important people in early Jefferson County. He was commissioned as a lieutenant colonel of the Jefferson County regiment of the Georgia militia on 13 October 1796[22] and remained at that rank until 26 February 1802 when he became a brigadier-general of the second brigade, first division of the Georgia militia.[23]

Not only was he active in military affairs, but he was also a very influential politician. He distinguished himself by his opposition to the Yazoo fraud, held many offices in the county, and was highly esteemed by his fellow citizens.[24] He was appointed as one of the judges of the Inferior Court of Jefferson County on 29 April 1796.[25] He also became a Georgia senator in 1796 and continued to be elected to this position until 1814.[26] He played an active role in the Georgia legislature and was also very popular with the people of Jefferson County.

Frequently he was not opposed for re-election, but when he was, he usually beat his opponent easily.[27] In the election of 1799 the senate race was between Solomon Wood, who received 418 votes, and Patrick Connolly, who received 8 votes.[28] The election of 1800 saw Wood beat Richard Gray 390 votes to 162 votes.[29] In the election of 1802 he had much stronger competition, but even then he received 343 votes while David McCormick received only 205.[30]

He lived to a goodly old age, but local tradition says that he fell from a wagon while making a trip to Augusta or Savannah to exchange produce for plantation supplies and sustained a broken leg, which caused blood poison, from which he died. He was buried on the high knoll near the old home site.[31]

When Solomon Wood died on 17 August 1815 at age fifty-seven, he left behind a large estate, his wife Elizabeth Eason Wood, and six living children (Green, Mark Red, John White, Nancy, Elizabeth, and Mary. In his will, which has been preserved at the Jefferson County courthouse, he divided his numerous possessions among his wife and children.

What he specified he was leaving behind for his wife is quite interesting:

> six Negroes to be her charge that is not named in my will, four horses and them to be her charge of all my stock and fifteen cows and calves, one yoke of stears and six stears for beef, accordance the stears, hogs, sheep and geese, six feather beds, furniture to be hers forever as her body live, all household furniture to be hers forever and at her disposure with the plantation whereon I now live with the things belonging there to be hers during her natural life also my stage wagon to be hers also.[32]

Noteworthy also is that he left for his children "five hundred dollars for their education."[33]

The Unusual Life of Joseph Gabriel Posner

One of the most interesting and colorful figures in the early history of Louisville was Joseph Gabriel Posner. The stories about Mr. Posner have held much fascination for many people in that they contain an aura of romance and mystery about them. Mr. Posner was a Polish Jew who had immigrated to Georgia early in its development. The first information about him comes from an advertisement in a Savannah newspaper of 20 November 1794 where notice is given that the copartnership of D'Lieben and Posner was being dissolved but that Joseph G. Posner would continue in the general merchandise store as sole owner.[34]

Exactly what happened to this business is not clear, but during 1795 Joseph Posner moved to Louisville. A 24 December 1795 advertisement in the *Georgia Gazette* gave the following information:

> The subscriber begs leave to inform his friends, and the public in general, that he has taken a very convenient house at Louisville, where a few gentlemen may be accommodated with board and lodging.[35]

Posner's boarding house became the main eating and meeting place in Louisville for the next twenty years. Many meetings were held in Mr. Posner's establishment and his "Long Room" became the most important meeting room in Louisville.[36] This room was large enough to seat at least eighty people for dinner.[37]

Not only did Joseph Posner have Louisville's most important boarding house, he also owned the largest general merchandise store in its early years. According to the Jefferson County tax digests of 1796 and 1801, his store had stock valued at $2,000 and $3,000 respectively.[38]

He was the representative of some companies in Louisville.[39] He also bought and sold extensive amounts of land in Louisville and Jefferson County[40] and handled some estates.[41]

Posner must have had his doubts about how the town of Louisville would fare when the capital moved away from there. A notice in the *Louisville Gazette and Republican Trumpet* in May of 1802 showed that he and James Meriwether were interested in making a change:

> To be sold or leased—for the term of five years—the commodious Houses and lots situated on the corner of Market Square, Louisville, (Metropolis of Georgia) whereon the subscribers now reside. The buildings are well calculated for stores and a Boarding House—For terms apply to Joseph G. Posner or James Meriwether.[42]

Apparently Mr. Posner did not sell his boarding house and restaurant until 1807, because a Roger Olmstead put an advertisement in the local newspaper, stating that he had

> taken that well know house in this place, formerly occupied by Joseph G. Posner, takes this method to acquaint all gentlemen travellers that he intends keeping a house of entertainment for planter, merchants, and other of a genteel cast on a plan which cannot fail to render general satisfaction.[43]

Mr. Olmstead may not have been successful in his endeavor and may have been forced to return the house to Mr. Posner, since an 1811 newspaper article mentions that the commissioners of the Ogeechee Navigation Company were holding their meetings at "Mr. Posner's long room."[44]

Joseph Gabriel Posner was the type of person who was always looking for a good investment. He apparently thought that he had found such an investment about twenty-eight miles from Louisville at Richmond Baths.[45] In the 21 May 1802 edition of the *Columbian Museum and Savannah Advertiser*, he notified the public:

that he has removed from the seat of government to this healthy and delightful place, where he prepares to keep a boarding house on an extensive plan for the accomadation of gentlemen & their families. The buildings here are indeed in a rough and unfinished state which he cannot remedy immediately nor will he engage to transplant the luxuries of the east to the west—Nothing, however in his power will be wanting to render the situation of those who favor him with their company as comfortable as possible—With wholesome fare, cold water, fare aid, sound wine and good cheer—who need fear the summer's heat or yellow-fever.---A few separate houses are now erecting and will be comfortably furnished on moderate rent, for the accommadations of gentlemen with their families.[46]

Just below this advertisement, and certainly a part of it, is an extract from a man in Augusta to a man in Savannah about the baths. It states that the baths are located near the main road from Augusta to Louisville about fourteen miles from the former,

in the midst of surrounding eminences, affording gratification to the eyes and health to the constitution. The baths, which already appear to be complete, are still, through the ingenuity of Mr. Posner, in a progressive state of improvement. In addition to a set of immersing and shower baths, supplied by a cold & pelucid [*sic*] fountain, he is erecting others in which the water may be used in any degree of temperature from cold to hot, and so contrived that these degrees may be regulated by the person using them so as to be most agreeable to the feeling or tributary to health.[47]

By the summer of 1803 Richmond Baths was in full operation. On 25 June 1803, Posner placed a long advertisement in the *Columbian Museum and Savannah Advertiser* in which he told about the facilities and prices. He mentioned that the baths at that time had one framed house with five rooms, and five other houses with two rooms each. There was also one large boarding house 60 x 36 that was two stories high and had two spacious public rooms and thirteen lodging rooms. There were also cold baths (two immersing and two shower) and six warm baths in separate apartments with dressing rooms. The prices for people to use this wonderful resort were as follows: board for a week $6.00; a servant for a week $2.50; horses for a week $3.00; lodging for one night $.12 1/2; dinner for one night $.50; Madierre wine per bottle $1.50; and $.25 for the use of the warm baths for one day.[48]

The English traveler Melish, who visited Louisville, also stopped at Richmond Baths on 6 July 1806 and gave the following report about his visit:

> Towards the spring, the country gets elevated, and agreeably uneven; but the soil is miserably poor. The springs have no other medicinal quality than what is covered by limestone, of which there is here a considerable bed; and there is a fine rivulet, which Mr. Posner, the proprietor, has very judiciously diverted into a bathing-house; and, at a great expense, has converted the whole into bathing quarters, with ample accomodations. I staid [I] two days at this place, and found my situation very comfortable. I had an opportunity of bathing in the pure spring water once or twice a day, and had limestone water, pure from the rock to drink. Our victuals were good, and the cookery excellent. My health I found reestablished, and my spriits recruited; so that every thing convurred [???] to render the place agreeable. And yet this place, which might be so beneficial to Georgia, is neglected.[49]

In February of 1811, Posner put another advertisement in a Savannah paper about his baths. The advertisement stated that

> the plunging baths are cut down through white stone; the floor being a solid rock. There are plunging showers and four warm baths for ladies—the same for Gentlemen—with a dressing room, to each part baths.

The situation there is described as being uncommonly dry and healthy, and the mineral spring was said to be very beneficial to "those who have had ocassion to drink the water." The price of board there was "one dollar per day—children half price—servants also fifty cents." If a place was rented by the month, the total price was twenty-one dollars. He also said that several small houses or lots were for rent or sale there.[50]

Apparently Joseph Posner spent a great deal of his money on Richmond Baths, and because people did not take advantage of the fine resort he had prepared, he ran into financial problems and lost much of his property. A Louisville newspaper of 1816 has an advertisement for a "Sheriff's sale" of the following property:

> 2 lots, nos. 241 and 242, with all the improvements thereon, adjoining Walnut and Eighth Streets; taken as the property of J. G. Posner &

Benedix, to satisfy and execution obtained on the foreclosure of a mortage, John Batton, surviving copartner, vs. Posner & Benedix.[51]

Joseph Posner was a highly respected man in the Louisville community and was public spirited. His name is even listed with the donors to Louisville's first church in 1810 even though he was Jewish. He gave fifteen dollars to this project and was one of the largest donors.[52]

Joseph Posner was also a poet. The following poem by Mr. Posner appeared in an 1804 edition of the Louisville newspaper:

> I have now returned to Louisville,
> Which is the place of my administration,
> Where I'll give good accomodation,
> And as good lodging and board
> As this country can afford.[53]

The English traveler Melish said of Posner's poetic abilities:

The old man is a sort of poet too, and, though his rhymes are not to be compared with those of Pope or Milton, yet they are humorously recited, and in a dialet [sic] that never fails to excite risibility. He favoured me with a copy of verses, which he addressed to a little swindling Jew of my acquaintance in Savannah, who, he said, had cheated him; and of which the concluding stanza will be sufficient to satisfy the reader of his poetical powers:

> But it surely was a great sin,
> To send me common whiskey
>   in place of Hollans gin.
> The worst remains behind,
> To send me common Malaga,
>   in place of good Madeira wine.[54]

Being such an active businessman and important person in the Louisville community, it is understandable that Mr. Posner would have some enemies. One of his enemies was Abner Hammond. In a letter to the editors of the *Louisville Gazette and Republican Trumpet* on 20 May 1800, Joseph Posner attacked a "malicious statement, with false assertions," of Abner Hammond against the firm of Posner and Benedix that had appeared in the 13 May 1800 edition of the paper.[55] Posner pointed out that Hammond had made "an extravagant charge of twenty one dollars for the labour of a negro for one month." He said this was done "only to over balance my account, which was justly due for money lent and advanced him." Posner further pointed out that he

> valued peace and quietness so high, as to consent to allow him all his ungenerous charges rather than be drawn into a quarrell with a person I was once blind enough to think a gentleman, but since had found him quite the reverse. He was mean enough to lay the same statement, which appeared in your last paper, before the grand jury of Jefferson County, last April court—and the grand jury finding no bill, the viper is biting the file still.[56]

An article in the *Colonial Museum and Savannah Advertizer* of 13 January 1797 makes it clear that Mr. Posner had other people in Louisville who did not like him.

> And on Thursday night last, fire was placed among some shavings under the store of Mr. Posner and blazed to a considerable height, but fortunately was extinguished without any material injury.[57]

As can be seen, Joseph G. Posner was an interesting and respected man who played a very important role in the Louisville community. One aspect about him, however, made him quite different from the other people of Louisville, yet the people there seemed to have accepted this fact and were very tolerant toward Mr. Posner. Joseph Posner had a slave by the name of Silvia by whom he produced a son David. At that time, it was contrary to custom, though not forbidden by law, for whites and blacks to marry. He was very devoted to David and Silvia, and he wished to avoid any legal difficulties for them. He made a special petition to the Georgia legislature to pass legislation freeing both of them. This law was passed in February of 1799 and read as follows:

> An act to manumit and exempt from certain penalties Sylvia and her son, David, now the property of Joseph Gabriel Posner. Whereas Joseph Gabriel Posner has by his petition presented to this present general assembly, prayed that Sylvia, a woman of color, and David her son, the property of Joseph Posner, should be manumitted and discharged from slavery et cetera.[58]

This act was passed in the house of representatives by a 35 to 14 vote.[59]
The English traveler Melish sadly noted that

> Mrs. Posner is a woman of colour, and is disliked by the Georgian
> ladies, who will not go to her house. Where the ladies will not go, the
> gentlemen will not go, and so poor Mr. Posner does not get a proper
> reward for his exertions, and the Georgians lose the benefit of one of
> the sweetest summer retreats in all the country.[60]

Unfortunately this family was not to stay together for very long. In
the 8 July 1800 edition of the *Louisville Gazette* a sad notice appeared
that Master David Sigmond Posner, the only son of Joseph G. Posner,
"died on July 4, 1800 being only 7 years, 5 months and 26 days old."[61]
Silvia and Joseph were to live together for many more years, but their
days were not always happy ones because of the death of this child and
the problems that Silvia experienced.

Mr. Posner established his wife Sylvia as the mistress of his home.
Sylvia was called "Mrs. Posner," and though she was not recognized
socially, she was respected for her good behavior. The story is told that
Mrs. Posner owned a parrot that held a wealth of fascination for the little
girls of Lousiville. They desired very greatly to see the parrot, but did not
dare to ask their parents' consent, knowing it would be denied. One day,
without asking, they visited the Posner home and were ushered in by a
maid. Mrs. Posner and the parrot took turns at conversing with the girls.
They later told their surprised mothers that Mrs. Posner was very kind to
them.[62]

Mr. Posner died several years before his wife, but prior to his death
local tradition says he built a large vault of brick and stone for himself
and for her in what is known as the Capital Cemetery of Louisville. He
requested his attorney to see that Sylvia was buried beside him.
According to tradition, this vault was above ground and quite imposing,
so much so that when portions of Sherman's army pillaged Louisville
they spotted the Posner vault and dug into it hoping that it contained
jewelry and/or money. All they found were the remains of a tragic
couple. Local tradition also says that some years later a cyclone struck
what was left of this pile of brick and stone and it was completely
destroyed so that no trace remains of the grave site today.[63]

As Joseph Gabriel Posner grew older, he realized that he should draw
up a will so that his wife and possessions could be protected. On 18
November 1812, he drew up a will in which he stated:

> I give, devise, and bequeath unto my well beloved wife Sylvia Sigmond Posner, all my estate both real and personal, what I now am, or may be possessed of at the time, of my death—for to have and to hold all that estate, both real and personal, during her natural life—and after her death, whatever part or portion of the said estate may be remaining undisposed of by her the said Sylvia Sigmond Posner it is my will and desire that it be disposed of and divided in manner and form following to wit.

Whatever part of the estate remained after Silvia's death, he willed one-third portions to "my brothers son (named) George P. Sigmond, the son of Dr. Joseph P. Sigmond, now living in Bath Somersetshir in the Kingdom of England," "to Gabriel Posner the son of Dr. David Posner (my brother) now living in the Kingdom of Poland and commonly called in that country the Reverend Doctor David, Son of Dr. Gabriel in Sheverzine near Posend" and to "the heirs of my sister Diana who may be living at the time of my death."[64]

Several years after he wrote his will, Joseph Posner died, leaving behind an estate appraised at $2,853.79. This estate included 5 slaves, 1 horse, 1 mule, 4 cows and calves, 7 hogs, 6 pigs, 4 turkeys, 6 ducks, 3 wagons and carriages, and a large quantity of furniture, books, and household items. Interestingly, in the inventory of his estate, no property is listed.[65] In the 1820 tax digest of Jefferson County, however, the estate of J. G. Posner was said to possess 5 slaves, lots in Louisville worth $1,000, and 1,000 acres of land.[66]

After the death of Joseph G. Posner, his wife Sylvia continued to live in the Lousiville area, but she was never accepted by the community. According to some Jefferson County records she was still living in the county at least as late as 1821. According to the 1819 tax digest, she owned a house and lot in Louisville worth $400 and paid $1.25 in property taxes.[67] While she was listed as a spinster in 1819, the Jefferson County records give her occupation as a "tavern keeper" in 1820 and 1821.[68] The 1819 "List of Free Blacks who Register in Jefferson County" also says that she was forty-five years old and was born in Georgia.[69]

Notes

[1]White, *Historical Collections*, 503.

[2]Farmer, "Early Religious Life of Jefferson County," 7.

[3]Robert Lathan, *History of the Associate Reformed Synod of the South* (Harrisburg PA, 1882) 284.

[4]Farmer, "Early Religious Life of Jefferson County," 7.

[5]*LG*, 2 July 1799; *LG*, 18 March 1800; *LGRT*, 5 November 1800 and 21 February 1801.

[6]Writings of Louisa M. Wright in the Jefferson County Library.

[7]Strickland, *Religion*, 179; Watkins, *Digest*, 615.

[8]Harriet Milledge Salley, ed., *Correspondence of John Milledge, Governor of Georgia, 1802-1806* (Columbia SC: The State Printing Co., 1949) 59; Notes from a Thesis by Mary Sanders Kilgore at the University of Georgia entitled "An Historical and Analytical Study of the Development of Schools in Jefferson County, Georgia."

[9]Letter from Rev. James Rodgers to Rev. David Bothwell on 2 January 1792 in the William W. Renwick Papers in the Duke University Library.

[10]*LGRT*, 4 July 1801.

[11]Farmer, "Early Religious Life of Jefferson County," 8.

[12]*LGRT*, 28 April 1802.

[13]Will of David Bothwell in Jefferson County Courthouse.

[14]Smith C. Banks Letter of 5 April 1970 in Jefferson County Library.

[15]Writings of Mary N. Anderson in the Jefferson County Library.

[16]Knight, *Georgia's Landmarks*, 704.

[17]Document in File II, Solomon Wood (Pre-1800) in the Georgia Department of Archives and History.

[18]*Thomas, History*, 26.

[19]Executive Council of Georgia Minutes, 21 May–16 December 1790, 161.

[20]*Jefferson County Tax Digest*, 1799.

[21]*Jefferson County Tax Digest*, 1814.

[22]*Executive Department Minutes*, 28 June 1798–6 February 1799, 252.

[23]Writings of Mary N. Anderson in the Jefferson County Library.

[24]Knight, *Georgia's Landmarks*, 704.

[25]*Executive Department Minutes*, 5 November 1793–23 September 1796.

[26]Writings of Mary N. Anderson in the Jefferson County Library.

[27]*LGRT*, 10 October 1801.   [28]*LG*, 8 October 1799.

[29]*LGRT*, 7 October 1800.   [30]*LGRT*, 27 October 1802.

[31]Thomas, *History*, 27.

[32]Will of Solomon Wood in Jefferson County Courthouse.

[33]Will of Soloman Wood in Jefferson County Courthouse.

[34]*Georgia Gazette*, 20 November 1794.

[35]*Georgia Gazette*, 24 December 1795.

[36]*Columbian Museum and Savannah Advertiser*, 14 February 1811; *SGLJ*, 24 December 1799.

[37]*LGRT*, 7 March 1801.

[38]*Jefferson County Tax Digests*, 1796 and 1801.

[39]*Georgia Gazette*, 21 April 1796. He represented the iron works of David Hillhouse in Franklin County.

[40]*LG*, 22 January 1799; *LGRT*, 27 May 1800; *LGRT*, 20 January 1802; *LGRT*, 26 May 1802; *LGRT*, 23 February 1803; *LGRT*, 8 August 1804; *LGRT*, 20 March 1807; *Executive Department Minutes*, 9 November 1799–4 November 1800, 222 and 236-38.

[41]*Georgia Gazette*, 1 January 1795; *SGLJ*, 24 Decmber 1799.

[42]*LGRT*, 12 May 1802.   [43]*LGRT*, 15 May 1807.

[44]*LG*, 2 February 1811.

[45]*Columbian Museum and Savannah Advertiser*, 23 April 1802.

[46]*Columbian Museum and Savannah Advertiser*, 21, May 1802.

[47]*Columbian Museum and Savannah Advertiser*, 21 May 1802.

[48]*Columbian Museum and Savannah Advertiser*, 25 June 1803.

[49]Melish, *Travels*, 46.

[50]*Columbian Museum and Savannah Advertiser*, 7 March 1811.

[51]*AA*, 23 May 1816.   [52]*News and Farmer*, 16 October 1930.

[53]*LGRT*, 17 October 1804.   [54]Melish, *Travels*, 46.

[55]*LGRT*, 13 May 1800.   [56]*LGRT*, 20 May 1800.

[57]*Columbian Museum and Savannah Advertiser*, 13 January 1797.

[58]Marbury and Crawford, *Digest*, 206; *Executive Department Minutes*, 6 February 1799–7 November 1799, 7 and 12.

[59]*House of Representatives Journal*, 6 February 1799, 50.

[60]Melish, *Travels*, 46.

[61]*LG*, 8 July 1800; *LGRT*, 23 February 1803. (Danielsville Heritage Papers, 1973)

[62]Lunita Segers Hardeman, *Reflections of Lights and Shadows in Georgia* (Danielsville: Heritage Papers, 1973) 15. Notebook of Mrs. Smith in the Jefferson County Library.

[63]Durden, *History*, 37.

[64]Will of Joseph G. Posner in the Jefferson County Courthouse.

[65]Inventory of the Estate of J. G. Posner in Jefferson County Courthouse.

[66]*Jefferson County Tax Digest*, of 1820.

[67]*Jefferson County Tax Digest*, of 1819.

[68]"List of Free Blacks who Register in Jefferson County" in 1819, 1820, and 1821 in Jefferson County Courthouse.

[69]"List of Free Blacks who Register in Jefferson County" in 1819 in Jefferson County Courthouse.

Appendix II
Interesting Articles in the Louisville Newspapers

The early newspapers of Louisville give an interesting picture of what the city and county were really like during "those glorious days." This appendix includes some of the articles that have been left out of the text of the book in the hope that they will help to give a better understanding of what was happening in Louisville and Jefferson County before, during, and after the capital was there.

An Important Indian Visitor

The people in Louisville and Jefferson County had experienced many problems with the Indians, and as late as 1788 Indians made a raid into Jefferson County in which they actually killed and scalped people. After Louisville became Georgia's capital, the leaders of the state sought to make peace with the Indians. They also wanted to obtain more land from the Indians so that Georgia settlers would have additional territory into which they could move. As a result of this desire, Indian chiefs were welcomed in Louisville and were even treated as honored guests. The 12 March 1799 edition of the *Louisville Gazette* contains an article about an Indian chief, one Cheehaw Mico, a leader of the Creek tribes, coming to visit Georgia's capital. The article appears as follows:

> On Monday, the 4th instant arrived in this town, the Cheehaw Mico, or King of one of the Creek Tribes. His visit was to the Governor, to procure payment for a horse, one of two which were stolen from him about six weeks since, over the Oconee River, by Peter Hutchinson and Merit Mitchell, two thieves, now safely lodged in the federal gaol, in Savannah. Hutchinson and Mitchell were apprehended with the other horse, by a party of militia sent after them, by the Governor, on their route to Tennessee and to prevent retaliation by the Indians, who threatened it, the Governor promised payment for the horse, which could not be recovered. On Tuesday the Governor paid him a talk, the substance of which was, that the Mico saw how just the white people were, that had received back one of his horses, and was paid for the other, and that the thieves were sent to gaol. That not withstanding this, two of the red people Cowetas, had crossed the Chulapocha, and killed white man, a Mr. John Moreland, while at work in his field—that as the

white people had done justice, so the Indians must do justice, and deliver the two Coweta murderers up—that a number of horses had been stolen along the frontier, and a number of negroes, belonging to citizens of Georgia, were in the nation—that they must be returned, or the chain of friendship would grow resty—that harboring run-away negroes bred ill blood between the two people. The Governor then told him he was glad he had placed as much confidence in him, as to come of his own accord at such a time, when the white people were angry about Moreland's death—that he was now in his power, but he might be easy—he was safe, it was not proper to punish the innocent for the gulty, and he would send an escort, and see him safe back over the River Oconee, and that he hoped he would fairly represent all the Governor had done for him, and said to him. The Mico then made a short answer, and promised to send in all the horses and negroes, which might come to his town—that he would go the Big council to be held in the nation, in April, and talk to the Chiefs on all he had seen and heard, and that he had no doubt but that Cowetas would be given up. Capt. Shellman's Louisville Artillery paraded on the occasion, and fired a salute; and the Indian King, with a number of Gentlemen, dined afterwards with the Governor. On Wednesday morning, the Chief having laid his money out in the stores of this place departed pleased, and well satisfied with the treatment he had received. We hope this proof of peace and freindship, shown by the State Government towards the Indians will whilst it wipes off those charges of creulty and hostility, which Georgians, have been so plentifully aspersed with—operate to induce the Creeks to give up the murderers of Moreland and to return the property of our fellow citizens. The Governor we understand wrote Col. Hawkins, some time past, demanding the murderers and has since received a letter informing him, that as soon as they were fixed on, it should be done.

Retirement Party for Governor Jackson

The people of Louisville liked to have parties and celebrations, particularly ones related to political figures and activities. One such party was given for Governor James Jackson on his retirement from office. *The Louisville Gazette and Republican Trumpet* of 7 March 1801 recorded the event as follows:

On Tuesday the 3d of March instant, a large number of the citizens of Jefferson County met at Mr. Posner's for the purpose of testifying their approbation of the administration of his excellency James Jackson, upon his retiring from office; Lt. Col. Solomon Weed was called to the chair, when an address in the words following was unanimously agreed to. Mr. Govert, Mr. Mounger, Mr. Shelman, Mr. Crawford and Mr. Lamar were appointed a committee to wait upon the Governor with the foregoing address. As a further testimony of the esteem for the administrative acts of the late Governor, were held in Jefferson County, an elegant entertainment was provided, and at three o'clock, Major Gen. Jackson, the President, Major Gen. Clarke, Brig. Gen. Morrison, the State and County Officers, and about 80 fellow citizens assembled at Mr. Posner's, and sat down to dinner; after which were given a whole series of toasts.

The Death and Funeral of Governor Jackson's Son

During the time that James Jackson was Governor in Louisville, he was very successful in his governmental activities, but he suffered considerable tragedy in his personal life. Two of his children died within a few months of each other. The death and funeral of one of his sons is described in an article in the *Louisville Gazette and Republican Trumpet* of 27 May 1800:

Died, on Tuesday last, the 20th instant, about noon, age 6 years 9 months and 16 days, Master John Milledge Jackson, the fourth son of our present Governor. The little amiable innocent a few minutes, ere stern death, put the solemn seal on his quivering lip, with, as it were a presentment of his approaching dissolution, asked from the afflicted father a last blessing, and from the grief worn mother a dying kiss. The parental benediction and salute received, instant, a darkning film the eye assailed, the fluttering pulse to vibrate ceased and the quickning spirit, to realms above ascended, leaving a clay cold corpse. On the following morning at ten o'clock, preceded by Mr. Gobert and Mr. Barron, with their respective scholars, and six young ladies dressed in white, the like number being pall bearers, and followed by the Governor, his three eldest children, and Master Whitfield; the state officers and a respectable and numerous train of the ladies and gentlemen of Loisville, the corpse was borne by the young gentlemen of the town alternately relieving each other to the burial ground, where the funeral service was performed, and expressive silent grief closed the awful scene.

How to Keep People Out of Your Garden

Apparently David M'Cormick was having trouble keeping people out of his garden, so he came up with a way that he thought would stop the garden trespassers. He wanted to make the whole community aware of his actions in the following ad in the *Louisville Gazette and Republican Trumpet* of 8 July 1802:

> The subscrier takes this public method of informing the owners of slaves in this place, that from the depredations lately committed on his garden, he is determined to put down a number of grass snakes, every night, the dreadful tendency of which, to those who tread on them, might be fatal; having no wish to injure the property of his fellow citizens, he has been induced to give this public notice.

Taxes on Carriages and Retailers

There were numerous taxes that people in Louisville and Jefferson County had to pay, and many times these taxes destroyed the taxpayers economically. Frequently there were notices about sales of property that had been taken by the tax collector because the owners were unable to pay. There were also notices at times about when and what taxes had to be paid. One such ad appeared in a 10 September 1799 edition of the *State Gazette and Louisville Journal*:

> The Duty on carriages and retailers, in Jefferson County will be received at the Office of Inspection in Louisville, from the 23rd to the last day of September, Sunday excepted. The duties are as follows: Upon every coach—$15, post Chariot—$15, post chaise—$12, phaeton with or without a top—$9, coaches—$9, other carriages having pannel work above with blinds, glasses or curtains—$9, four wheel carriages having framed posts and tops with steel springs—$6, four wheel top carriages with wooden or iron springs or jacks—$3, curricles with tops— $3, chaises with tops—$3, two wheel carriages with steel or iron springs—$3, other two wheel carriages—$2, four wheel carriages having framed posts and tops and resting upon wooden spars—$2. Applications for licences for retailing spirits and wines will be received at the same time and place. Thomas Collier, Collector of the Revenue, Sixth Division, First Survey in the District of Georgia.

Building a Church in Louisville

As was mentioned in the main part of the book, Louisville had no church until 1811. The local newspaper carried a notice about what decisions were being made about the church and how the money was being raised to build it. The following appeared in the *Louisville Gazette* of 4 May 1810:

> At a meeting of the commissioners to erect a house of pulic worship in the town of Louisville, May 4, 1810. Present John Berrien, Chairman, Mr. Robinson, Mr. Scott, Mr. Harman. On motion resolved that the subscribers be requested to pay into the hands of the treasurer, Mr. William N. Harman, their several subscriptions immediately, so as to enable the commissioners to proceed in making their contract—and that the subscribers be publicly notified in the Louisville Gazette, to come forward and pay their several subscriptions, by or before the 29th of the present month. Resolved, that the building of a house of public worship shall be forty feet in length and thirty in breadth—and that a particular plan of the same be lodged with the secretary of the board, Mr. Day, for the purpose of receiving proposals for building the same, the former plan being considered too large.

Charge to and Presentments of a Grand Jury

The Grand Jury played a very important role in the life of Louisville and Jefferson County. In many ways it was the overseer of ethics, morality and lawfulness. Important citizens were selected to serve on this jury and their presentments were highly respected and usually followed. In the *Louisville Gazette and Republican Trumpet* 7 April 1802, the charge of Judge Walton to the Grand Jury of Jefferson County was given as well as the presentments that resulted from the Grand Jury investigation. Judge Walton's charge was printed as follows:

> Considering that the policy of our government, has assigned to you the appellate and equitable jurisdiction in civil cases, in addition to the ancient and inestimable privilege of criminal inquisition; being also informed, that the callender or the latter ground, is small in comparison with the weight of buisness apparent on the docquets; and being desirous of removing the idea that it is neither expected or essential to enter on business the first day of the term—I say, for these reasons, I

yesterday dispensed with the usual practice of addressing you upon the first opening of the Court; and of your being impannelled—and sworn, in order to proceed in calling the docquets; and I have the pleasure to add, that, although some little impediments occurred, a respectable portion of buisness was got through. I will therefore, be hence forward understood by all, and particularly by parties and there, that business will commence with the term. It is, that I might expoain myself onthis ground, and to make the declaration I have just done; as well as from the respect due from members of the Superior Courts, that I have thought it necessary to address you at all at present. In the habit of disscharging similar duties with those you are now called upon to attend to, you want, not to be instructed how act. From the practice of the social virtues public integrity naturally results; and the part you are to take on the present occasion will be tempered with justice, and governed by firmness. I cannot conclude this short address, without felicitating you, and my fellow citizens at large, on the present happy and tranquil state of our internal administration. We see a citizen placed in chair state, being of no party, and of course neither exciting or attaching envy or enmity; and before whose mild and just administration the voice of sanction ceases to be here—such is the reality of a free government.

In response to this charge, the Grand Jury did its investigation and made the following presentments:

1st. We present as a great grievance that the Roads and Bridges throughout this county are not kept in better repair; they are generally so narrow and extremely bad; they are almost impassible for waggons loaded with cotton the staple commodity of this country, and recommend it to proper authority to take notice thereof.

2nd. We particularly present it as a grievance, that the bridge across the Ogechee River, known as Page's Bridge, and kept as a toll bridge, is not kept in sufficient repair for the safe passage of travellers.

3rd. We present William M'Gehee and Catherine Wallace for living in adultery.

4th. We present John Coleman and Mary Ford, for living in adultery.

5th. We present as a grievance, the unlawful practice of hunting in the night with fire light, by which much damage has been done in this county, by setting fire to the woods and communicating it to the fences of the plantations, and destroying them, and recommend it to the justices of the different districts to be vigilant in discovering offenders of this kind; and also recommend a more strict attention to the patrole law, which has been hitherto much neglected.

6th. We present Thomas Gibson, for unlawfully setting fire to the woods, from which several individuals have received some damage.

7th. We present it as a grievance, that the law prohibiting profane swearing is not better executed.

Learning that the State of South Carolina has purchased Messrs. Miller and Whitney's patent right of their cotton machines, and thus free'd its citizens from expensive and litigious suits, as well as a burdensome tax exacted from them by the patentees, we conceive that considerable advantages would result to the citizens of this state from a similar purchase, and therefore recommend it to the Legislature as an object worthy of their attention, but are of opinion that they ought not exceed the sum of $25,000, as the quantity of cotton raised in this state, is far less than that of our sister state.

We thank his Honor the Judge for his assiduity to the duties of his office, and his polite charge, and join with him in expressing our approbation of the present chief Magistrate being charged with the administration of our government, without detracting from the merit of his predecessors; and recommend that our presentments, together with the Judge's Charge be published as usual. Benj. Whitaker, Foreman, Robert Montgomery, David Emanuel, jun., Zachariah Lamar, Samuel Bothwell, John Shellman, Stephen Johnson, Joseph Hampton, James Neely, Arthur Cheatham, Joseph Allen, John Darby, John Fore, John Moreland, Isaac Coleman, John Cowart, John Cobbs, A. Love, R. Flournoy, Thacker Vivion and R. Shelman, Clerk.

Appendix III
Interesting Materials in the Tax Digest

Much can also be learned about the people who lived in Louisville and Jefferson County and the economy of the area by looking at the early tax digests. In this appendix the people who lived in the military district where Louisville was located in 1796 and 1814 will be listed and the people who owned lots and/or houses in Louisville will also be given.

The people listed in the Louisville District by the *Jefferson County Tax Digest* of 1796 are as follows: Enoch Walker; Henry Caldwell; Josiah Stirett; Thos. Ringland; Joseph G. Posner; Michael Shelman; Blasm. Harvey; Francis Brown; Thos. Pebbles; Jon. Pugsley; Chas. Gachett; John Bostick; Hugh Lambert; Thos. Collins; Joseph Chairs; Peter Williamson; John Fore; Wm. Evans; John Downer; Daniel Eubank; John Mackey; Robt Stone; John Stephenson; Robert Warnock; Lindsay Coleman; Thomas Lawson; Betsey Parmor (widow); Henry Cox; John Gill; Lewis Voule; Wm. McGehee; Lewis McCoy; Chesley Bostick, Jr.; David Jameson; Jon. Lewis; Jas. Stubbs, esq.; Mathew Carswell; John Manson; Blass. Thomas; Wm. Parsons; Jon. Parsons; Jas; Parsons; Jas. Woodburn; Roger Lawson; Henry Wall; Jon. Wilson; Benj. Whitaker; Jon. Barron; Richd. Womach; Wm. Betty; Sam. Betty; Jas. Wilson; Daniel Sturges; Daniel Thomas; John Tomkins; David Clem; David McGowan; Wm. Asque; Benj. Browning; Alex. Carswell; Wm. Hart; Robt. Mucklejohn; Thos. Tanner; Wm. Manson; Isaac Rawls; Ezel. Karr; Henry Shaffer; Joseph Rees; Fredrick Clem; Ephraim Pebbles; George Eubanks; Thos. Johnson; Hugh Kenealy; Wm. Clarke; Jas. Manson; Hugh Gilmore; Wm. Cohoon; Jon Ponsheer; Henry W. Williams; Jas. Brandon; Stephen M'Coy; Henry Pendleton; Michl. Schley; John Scott; John Prescott; John Rogers; John Allen; Wm. Black; Robt. Black; Wm. Fleming; Blass. Harvey, Jr.; Wm. Hadden Sr.; Wm. McDowel; David Bothwell; Chesley Bostick, Sr.; Wm. Barron; John Dixon; David Walker; James Merriwether; Philip Clayton; Francis Flanders; John Berrien; Horatio Marbury; Benj. Powell; John Parsons; Sam. Jordan; Henry Jordan; Arthur Jordan; John Shelma, esq.; and James Bozeman.

Those people who owned lots and the number of lots they owned, according to the 1796 tax digest are as follows: Enoch Walker (1); Josiah Stirett (2); Joseph G. Posner (1); Mich. Shelman as Trustee for Peter Clyma and Wm. Wash (11); Chas. Gachett (3); John (1); Thomas Collins

(1); Joseph Chairs (3); John MacKey(one-half); Lindsay Coleman (2); Betsy Parmor(widow) (2); Wm. McGehee (5); Chesley Bostwick, Sr. (4 and one-half); Thos. Stubbs, esq.(5); Thos Woodburn (1); Tom Barron (2); Daniel Sturges (1); Wm Hart for Dr. Tom B. Rusten (4); Isaac Rawls (1); Frederick Clem (1); Wm. Clarke (2); Henry W. Williams (1); Thos. Brandon (one-half); John Scott (11); John Prescott (1); Wm. Black (2); Wm. Fleming (1); Wm. McDowell (2); Chesley Bostick, Sr. (2); Wm. Barron (1); John Dixon (2); James Merriwether (3); Philip Clayton (1); John Berrian (3); John Parsons (6); John Shelman, esq. Trustee (6); Tom Lewis (4); Tom Rowland (1); Elijah Padgett (1); R. G. Christian (1) and David Terry (1).

The list of the people living in the Louisville district, called the Fokes' District in the *Jefferson County Tax Digest* of 1814, is as follows: Samuel Barron; John Fores; Gideon Willis; Jesse Jones; William McFarland; Stephen Minton. L. Penington; Beniah Carswell; Jesse Robinson; Hudson Raglen; Simeon Spivey; Michael Burke; Emanuel Hammock; John Coleman; Samuel Clarke; Shedracke Rawles; Daniel Eubanks; John Parsons; Simpson Chance; Elijah Hutchin; Manson chance; Job Tounsley; John Kelly; Elijah Sutton; Dr. Josian M. Sterrett; William Lockhart; David Clarke; Isom McClendon; James Meriwether; William McClendon; James Clarke; Lemuel Drake; John Eubanks; Isaac Rawles, Sr.; William Fokes; David Rozier; Joseph Hall; Dr. B. D. Thompson; Thomas Hancock; Anthony Hancock; Leon H. Marks; Starling Jordan; William Batty; Joseph White; Benamiel Bower; Robert Herring; Margaret Cudy; David McConky; Jacob McCullough; Robert Willis; Eli M. A. Cassille; Michael Shelman; William Wright; Robinson Asque; Lemuel Taylor; John King; Abram Robinson; William Hadden; Michael Schley; Bob Martin; John Guyton; John Smith; Joseph Martin; Sarah Prince; Margaret Whitley; Wyriatt Cason; Daniel Lemle; William Gilliam; James C. Blount; Archibald Campbell; Sanders Burnet; Ann M. Maxwell; Daniel Furguson; Thomas Paulett; Isaac Rawls, Jr.; Suseen Whidbee; John I. Schley; William N. Harman; George Eubank; John Gordon; Thomas M. Berrien; John Schley; John Paulette; Arthur Clarke; William Schley; Andrew Moore; Dr. John Powell; John P. Harvey; Robert Lowden; Moses Smith; Littleberry Bostick; Frederick Harris; James Smith; Ambrose Wright; Galphin Harvey; John Cox; Robert Jones; John Tripp; Susannah Perkins; Sarah Burke; James Chance; Tandy Jones; John Berrien; Willis Gorham; William Robinson; Eliza W. Jackson; Alexander Meriwether; Etheldred Moore; Edward T. Salter; Lewis Sutton; and Fountain Eubanks.

Although the 1814 tax digest does not give the number of lots owned, it does gives the names of people who owned lots in Louisville and they are as follows: Ambrose Wright; Littleberry Bostick; Tardy C. Key; John P. Harvey; Dr. John Powell; Andrew Moore; J. G. Posner; William Schley; Arthur Clarke; John Schley; John Gordon; William N. Harman; John J. Schley; Ann M. Maxwell; Archibald Campbell; Marget Whitley; Sarah Prince; Michael Schely; William Hadden; Elizabeth Augue; Henry Mears; William Wright; Michael Shelman; Eli M. Cassille; David McConky; Margaret Cudy; Roert Fleming; Samuel White; William Batty; Strislling Jordan; Thomas Handcock; David Rozier; James Merriwether; David Clarke; Dr. Josiah M. Sterrett; L. Sykes Tounsley; Job Tounsley; John Parsons; John Willia; Mary Fenn; Philip Scott; Baldwin Raiford; Benj. Davis; Winford Ronaldson; James Powell; Dr. John Pugsley; David Bothwell Jr.; Ebenezer Bothwell; John Hammath; James Batey; William Hayles; and John Bostick.

The changes in population were dramatic between 1796 and 1814 in Louisville. Although the number of people listed in the tax digests remained almost exactly the same (110 in 1796 and 111 in 1814), the names of the people changed greatly. Either because of death or relocation, there were only ten people who were listed in both of these tax digests. They were Daniel Eubanks; John Parsons; Dr. Josiah Sterrett; James Merriwether; William Batty; Michael Shelman; Michael Schley; George Eubanks and John Berrien. The family names of some people continued in Louisville even though the same individual was not there. These continuing family names; ten in number; were Barron; Carswell; Coleman; Clarke; Rawls; Powell; Bostick; Harvey; Cox; and Asque.

As can be seen very few of the Louisville families of 1796 were still present in Louisville in 1814. In fact, only 9% of the people listed in the 1796 tax digest were still on the list in 1814, and only 18% of the 1796 family names appeared in 1814. This clearly shows the tremendous population change as Louisville shifted from an economy centered around the state government to one centered around agriculture.

The same is true of the people who owned lots in Louisville in 1796 and in 1814. In 1796 there were only forty-one lot owners in Louisville. This number increased to fifty-one in 1814. This increase in lot owners was probably due to the selling of additional lots in Louisville and the selling of lots by some people who owned multiple lots in 1796. Of the forty-one who owned lots in 1796, only four of them still owned lots in 1814 (J. G. Posner, Michael Shelman, James Merriwether, and John Parsons). This is only 9% of the 1796 group. There were also four other families who continued to own lots even though the original owner was not listed. These families were Clarke, Fleming, Bostick, and Scott. They make up only 19% of the original families owning lots in Louisville. These percentages agree almost exactly with those from the tax digest listing of people who lived in Louisville and also show the extreme population changes that took place in Louisville as "those glorious days" ended and Louisville adjust to its loss of "capital status."

Index

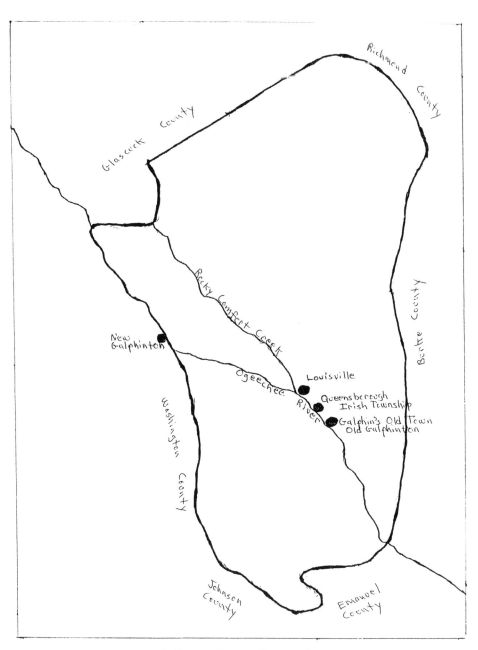

Jefferson County Historic Sites